Issues of New Testament Anti-Judaism

Son of Man, Deicide, and Divine Predetermination

Roger Steven Evans

University Press of America,® Inc.
Lanham · Boulder · New York · Toronto · Plymouth, UK

Copyright © 2008 by
University Press of America,® Inc.
4501 Forbes Boulevard
Suite 200
Lanham, Maryland 20706
UPA Acquisitions Department (301) 459-3366

Estover Road
Plymouth PL6 7PY
United Kingdom

All rights reserved
Printed in the United States of America
British Library Cataloging in Publication Information Available

Library of Congress Control Number: 2008905609
ISBN-13: 978-0-7618-4143-2 (paperback : alk. paper)
ISBN-10: 0-7618-4143-1 (paperback : alk. paper)
eISBN-13: 978-0-7618-4225-5
eISBN-10: 0-7618-4225-X

∞™ The paper used in this publication meets the minimum
requirements of American National Standard for Information
Sciences—Permanence of Paper for Printed Library Materials,
ANSI Z39.48—1984

This book is dedicated to my wife, Christine.

CONTENTS

Preface	vii
Acknowledgements	ix
Introduction	xi
Chapter 1: Conflict in the Gospels	**1**
The "Son of Man" as the Messiah	1
The Messiah in First Century Judaism	2
The "Son of Man" in the Q Gospel	5
The "Son of Man" in the Gnostic Writings	8
The "Son of Man" as Jesus' Most Common Self-Identifying Term	9
The "Son of Man" in the Canonical Gospels	10
Conclusion	32
Chapter 2: Conflict in the Book of Acts and the Canonical Epistles	**43**
The Book of Acts	44
The "Jews" in Acts	44
Charges of Blasphemy in Acts	45
The Canonical Epistles	46
The Case of the Apostle Paul	46
Paul's Preaching in Acts	47
The Jewish Targets of Paul's Preaching in Acts	47
The Jewish Reactions to Paul's Preaching in Acts	50
Paul's Attempt to Rewrite Israel's History	51
Chapter 3: Deicide, Divine Predetermination, and Deliverance in the New Testament	**55**
Sacred Texts the Charge of Deicide	56
The Charge of Deicide in the Gospels	57
The Charge of Deicide in Acts	58
The Charge of Deicide in the Epistles	65
Divine Predetermination in the Epistles	66
Hope for Israel's Salvation	69
The Book of Acts	69
The Pauline Epistles	72
Conclusion	76
Chapter 4: Conclusion	**81**
Bibliography	85
Index	93
Scripture	93
Name	94
Subject	95
About the Author	97

Preface

Gospels and epistles, both canonical and Gnostic, monographs, letters, sermons, interviews, commentaries, poems, apologies, and laws are a sampling of the genre of Christian literature from the first six centuries of the common era that either explicitly or incidentally attempt to deal with Jewish spirituality or the Jewish religion, history, culture, tradition or people. Some of these works are fairly well known to scholars of early Christianity, but as I did research for my class, *Christianity and Judaism: A History of Conflict*, I discovered that both the scope and depth of this conflict, at least from the Christians, was far more extensive than I imagined. At first, the discoveries of this vast literature were almost accidental, but as I continued to happen upon these documents, I began to collect them as resources for a book. *En masse* they constitute an *Adversus Judaios*, which many scholars, both Jewish and Christian, believe sets the stage for the centuries of hostilities that have, both in the East and West, often broken out into pogroms, mass deportations, forced conversions, and sponsored and random slaughters.

Of course, all of these documents (listed in the bibliography) were preceded by or were written contemporaneously with the books that eventually made it into the Christian canon. Therefore, when I began to write this book, I envisioned including a chapter on the New Testament. However, it soon became apparent that the issues of anti-Judaism and/or anti-Semitism in the New Testament could not possibly be thoroughly explored in just one chapter.

Beginning with the Gospels, I discovered that many (though not all) of the incidents between Jesus and the Jewish leaders took place in the context of Jesus speaking of Himself as the "Son of Man." In these texts, Jesus is portrayed unmistakenly as the Messiah, and not just a Messiah that has divine prerogatives, but who is actually divine, viz., ἐγώ εἰμί (Jhn 8.58). Therefore although there were other issues concerning understandings of the Torah—principally issues of hermeneutic—it was the charge of blasphemy that led to the final conflict between Jesus and the Jewish leaders.

As told by the writers of Acts of the Apostles and the authors of the epistles, the cataclysmic event of the crucifixion is laid at the feet of the Jewish people who are accused then of deicide. This charge soon becomes the theological *raison d'etre* for the theological hatred of the Jewish people despite the repeated attempts by Jesus to tell the apostles that He and His Father sent Him as a sacrifice for sin. In reading the Acts of the Apostles and the epistles, neither the Roman governor Pilate, King Herod, nor God carried any responsibility for the crucifixion. This has received the attention of scholars before now, but an analysis needed to be repeated in this context again.

Finally, especially for those who will want to use the New Testament to support God's rejection of the Jews, a careful reading of the work of Paul and the reception of his preaching and teaching as recorded in the book of Acts reveals the first Christians continually reaching out to their Jewish neighbors.

Roger Steven Evans
Pickerington, Ohio
January, 2008

Acknowledgements

I want to thank my son Aaron, who read parts of the manuscript and helped me work through some knotty theological questions and who helped with some matters of formatting; Dr. Solomon Avotri, who helped me understand some of the questions and history of the Q Gospel; and Ms. Marcy Thorner for her work in formatting and editing.

Finally, I want to thank my students at Payne Seminary, who always seem to ask the questions I am not expecting.

Introduction

In the four Christian canonical gospels, Jesus of Nazareth seemed to have almost constant contact with Jewish religious leaders in Palestine following the beginning of His public ministry (Mk 2.1–12; Lk 4.16–30; Jhn 2.13–30).[1] There is a long-standing Christian hermeneutic that suggests that the conflicts that arose from these early encounters are the initial stages of the ever-heightening hostility between Jesus and His followers, and the Jewish leaders and their supporters that led to a regrettable end; the crucifixion of Jesus. However, it can also be argued that the disputes themselves are not evidence of anything other than disputes between two opposing hermeneutic of the Jewish sacred literature. David Rokeah writes that in these encounters, though the "dominant note is still negative and hostile . . . one may find positive statements favorable toward the Jewish people and the Jewish Torah expressed in the Gospels."[2] What is found in many of these gospel passages are Jewish leaders questioning Jesus about what they perceived as "unorthodox" teachings. These ranged from His teachings on the Sabbath (Mt 12.1–8; Lk 10.10–14; Jhn 5.1–13),[3] to His claims of a special relationship to God (Mt 26.62–65. cf. Mk 14.53–65; Lk 22.54–65; Jhn 5.15–18; 18.12–24), to His teaching concerning the Tanakh[4] or the Torah[5] (Mt 5.17; 23.23; Jhn 7.19–23), or ones that they simply did not understand, that is, being born again (Gr = $ἄνωθεν$ = "from above"; Jhn 3.3) to giving His flesh to eat (Mt 26. 26–29; Jhn 6.51–59). Read (and perhaps written) from an adversarial per-spective, many Christian readers of the New Testament have come to believe that the Jewish leaders' requests for either signs or questions about under whose authority Jesus operates (Mt 21.23–27) were plottings of the Pharisees to "entan-gle [Jesus] in His talk" (Mt 22.15; cf. Mk 12.13–17; Lk 20.20–26).[6] Yet these questions directed at Jesus and His disciples may also be seen as perfectly legitimate questions of men who were the appointed and accepted spiritual and religious leaders of the Jewish people in both Palestine and the Jewish Diaspora. Further, many of the moral teachings that Jesus directed to either the leaders or the general populace are moral teachings with which many of the leaders themselves would readily agree. However when they are spoken by someone whom the leaders perceived as a threat, and/or by someone who did not have any apparent formal religious training (Jhn 7.15), the reception of these teachings cannot be expected to be accepted with open arms, and were, in fact, resisted.[7]

A study, then, of the possibility of anti-Judaism in the New Testament should begin with an analysis of the canonical gospels, which are held by many Christians to be the most reliable retelling of the story of Jesus.[8] However, before an analysis of these texts can begin, questions of authorship must first be addressed, and how these questions are answered depends on beginning presuppositions. Opinions vary widely, from those who believe in a literal, verbal inspiration to the one expressed by John Meagher, who writes,

> Both the Jesus movement and the rabbinic movement told tales intended to validate their respective positions by substituting fairy-tale story for history. Neither side is much to be trusted in either the adequacy of its information or the shape of its story. Both have contributed importantly to the confusion that continues to make critical investigation troublesome.[9]

Bruce Chilton writes that in the four canonical gospels, as well as the Gospel of Thomas, "Judaism and the Jews appear more as a foil for Jesus than as the matrix of his movement," implying a motive to the storytelling that twisted the stories for polemical purposes.[10]

It is, however, perhaps a less argumentative position that can be used as the starting point for an attempt at exegesis. It is fair to say that many New Testament scholars accept the axiom that the four canonical gospels began with oral and written traditions, with a form of the Q Gospel being a common ancestor to Matthew and Luke.[11] Others may argue other theories, but the point that can be made is that the canonical gospels began with ever-changing oral and written traditions. Some of these changes may have been unintentional, but scholars suggest that others may have been purposeful.[12] The canonical gospel stories, then, that made it into print may or may not fully represent the events in the experiences in the life of Jesus, including His encounters with the Jewish leaders. In other words; are the hostilities between Jesus and the religious leaders the work of later redactors, or remembrances of Matthew and John, and the stories heard by Mark and Luke? Marvin Perry and Frederick Schweitzer write that by the time the New Testament was canonized (c. 380), what we have are "transcripts of transcripts of transcripts."[13] Elaine Pagels and Karen King write, "It is highly unlikely that any of [the canonical gospels] were written by disciples who personally knew Jesus, but we do not know who actually wrote them."[14] The profundity, then, of how one answers questions about the authorship of the gospel accounts of the encounters of Jesus and the religious leaders will be discussed later, but it is a question that comes before the texts can be exegeted.

Perhaps the most commonly accepted presupposition of conservative scholars is that the four canonical gospels were finally penned by the apostles Matthew and John, and the disciples Mark and Luke. Their sources include oral and written traditions passed along or gathered together supplemented with their own remembrances.[15] Beginning with these possibilities, the stories of the encounters between Jesus and the Jewish leaders can be read in the following ways:

A) The stories, events, and encounters of Jesus and his followers with the Jewish leaders found in the Gospels are faithful witnesses of the events as they are remembered. Modern interpreters who begin with this presupposition will need to decide how to read the stories of conflict between Jesus and the religious leaders. There are a number of options:

1) The conflicts between Jesus and the Jewish leaders were examples of internecine conflicts that have bedeviled religious groups for hundreds of years. This interpretation allows the reader either to:

a) Look at these conflicts through the eyes of the Jewish leaders and attempt to empathize with their understandable resistance to this self-proclaimed Messiah who had no credentials and did not meet what had become common expectations of the coming Messiah. In this interpretation (not seen in early Christian texts), the Jewish leaders are guilty of nothing.

b) Read these stories in light of the rest of the Gospel stories, which often speak of the love, compassion, and desire of Jesus Christ for all of mankind, including the Jewish people (see Mt 1.21; 10.5–13; 11.28–30; 18.11–14; 22.1–14; 28.19; Jhn 3.16; 6.35–58; 17.20—26). In this interpretation, the Jewish leaders are merely examples of people who, throughout history, have decided not to accept who Jesus claimed to be. While millions of Christians from the first century to today have accounted this as a sin, it can be argued that the Jewish leaders are still guilty of nothing.

c) Believe the asides of the Gospel stories, which constantly question the motives and intentions of the Jewish religious leaders in their hostility and resistance to Jesus and His teachings. In this interpretation, the Jewish leaders are guilty not only of resisting God and God's Sent Messenger, but of plotting and participating in His murder.

2) The conflicts are part of a pattern of rejection of the Messiahship of Jesus, which culminated in the crucifixion. The Jewish leaders in this interpretation are guilty of being, in the eyes of the New Testament authors, "stiff-necked."

3) The third possible interpretation reads something like this: If the words put into the mouth of Jesus Christ are His and are understood as declaring the Jewish leaders as hopelessly recalcitrant and lost, then His followers, believing Jesus to be God incarnate and wishing to imitate Him (Jhn 20.21), would have no problem following His attitude (Phil 2.5) and echoing these condemnations. And although this is not an uncommon interpretation of the Gospel

stories, Jesus is never heard unilaterally condemning the Jewish people, and, in fact, one of his last prayers to His Father is that they be forgiven (Lk 23.34).[16] The Jewish leaders, believing they were ridding their people of another politically and theologically troublesome teacher, would not understand the request of Jesus from God to forgive them.

Complicating all interpretations of these encounters are the events surrounding the crucifixion, which require more demanding and careful analyses. In other words, if the conflicts between Jesus and the Jewish leaders ended before the crucifixion, or if Jesus had ended his ministry in a different manner, that is, dying a peaceful death, or being taken back up to heaven or simply disappearing from the scene, then an analysis of the conflicts between Jesus and the religious leaders would be quite different. But that is not an option for those who believe the four canonical gospels are faithful remembrances of the events of both the life and death of Jesus. For those Christians, the crucifixion must be addressed. Loyd Gaston writes, "A New Testament without the Christ-event . . . would not be the New Testament at all."[17] Rosemary Ruether, beginning from an assumption that the Apostles rejected official forms of Judaism states it differently:

> Until the actual moment of Jesus' death, one cannot really speak of a trauma of rejection as fundamentally conditioning the attitude of the disciples toward official Jewish tradition. But this is to say that, prior to this trauma of Jesus' death, one cannot speak of Christian faith at all, but only of those preconditions that prepared for the revelatory moment. . . . Up until [the moment of the crucifixion], there was always the possibility (for the disciples, for the "crowds," and even for the official leadership) of a miracle. If he were really the Messiah, God would rescue him from impending disaster, overthrow his enemies, and vindicate His prophet in some miraculous intervention that would show that Jesus' word was an intrinsic part of God's plan for the coming of the Kingdom. But instead, Jesus dies, was buried in a borrowed grave, and to most eyes, no miracle occurred.[18]

Just as the earlier conflicts between Jesus and the religious leaders allow a number of interpretations, so the events of the crucifixion can also be seen in a number of ways:

A) The Jewish leaders, in league with the Roman appointed King Herod and the Roman ruler Pontius Pilate are guilty of deicide and stand condemned before God.

B) The Jewish leaders, in league with Herod, the Roman ruler, were simply the agents used by God and Jesus Christ Himself to fulfill what Jesus repeatedly told His disciples, both directly and indirectly, that He had come to the earth to do, that is, die for their sins (see Mt 1.21; 9.15; 16.21; 17.22–23; 20.17–19; 26.1-2, 26–42, 52-56; 27.35). In this interpretation, to hold the Jewish leaders accountable for what God had intended to do through Jesus Christ requires a God who plunges His own chosen people into a theological and condemnational abyss from which there may be no escape.

There are some interpreters who believe that although the gospels were written by Matthew, Mark, Luke, and John, that some or all of the encounters of

Jesus and the Jewish leaders are the works of later redactors. The possible motivations for such interpolations could include a genuine hatred of the Jewish leaders for their part in the crucifixion of Jesus, a hostility toward the Jews for their perceived rejection of Jesus as the promised Messiah, or an early attempt to demonstrate to Roman officials and potential pagan converts that the followers of Jesus are not another Jewish sect but members of an entirely different religion. There is external, non-canonical evidence that all of these understandings emerged and grew as the post-crucifixion relationships between the followers of Jesus and the Jewish leaders disintegrated.[19] If the editorializing of the encounters are later interpolations, then they cannot belong to Matthew, Mark, Luke, and John and reveal a hostility toward the Jewish religion (anti-Judaism) and/or the Jewish people (anti-Semitism), by later followers of Jesus, but not necessarily of the Apostles. This argument may be strengthened by the almost total absence of hostile encounters between Jesus and the Jewish leaders in the Q Gospel, a source for Matthew and Luke.[20]

Further, if some of the encounters are later redactions, we would need to know which ones are, for not all of the encounters are of the same type. Further, although many attempts have been made to identify these later redactions, there is no agreement as to which, if any, are. Claudia Setzer observes that as the composition of the gospels developed, several levels emerged:

> The pre-Markan level recalls disputes in the early church over the relative authority of oral traditions, the Markan compositional level that combines memories of those disputes with Mark's interpretation of them and their meaning for his community, and the Matthean level, where disputes over the oral law again come to the fore.[21]

Douglas Hare argues that "from a careful study of the development of the synoptic tradition it is clear that 'scribes' and/or 'Pharisees' or 'high priests' have been added to controversy stories in which the opponents of Jesus were originally unspecified."[22] Ruether agrees and says that as "hostility toward the Pharisees [grew] the word 'Pharisee' was now added to controversy stories where previously there had been unnamed or earlier opponents."[23]

While none of the gospels are exempt from the editorializing that has been used by Christians throughout their history to defame the first century Jewish leaders, some have identified the Gospel of Matthew as the most polemical. Bruce Chilton writes, "The Matthean Jews are liars in respect to the resurrection (28.15), and willful murderers who implicate their own children in the crucifixion (27.25).[24] Meager says that Pharisaic Judaism "came under heavy fire from Matthew" and that Matthew "seems vexed . . . by the failure of the Jews to recognize their messiah."[25] Scott McKnight agrees and says that "Matthew is arguing directly against nonmessianic Judaism and can therefore be accurately classed as reflecting 'anti-nonmessianic Judaism' or anti-disobedient Judaism."[26] Looked at from this perspective, McKnight refuses to name the Gospel of Matthew anti-Semitic, but his polemic is simply an "inheritance from Jewish polemic" and that many religious groups in the ancient world used "extremely volatile language expressing group differentiation and, through differentiation, identification."[27] He further points out that L. T. Johnson sees the New Testament polemic as "remarkably mild" in contrast to Hellenistic conventions. On the other hand, M. J. Cook believes that "some of the statements of the New Testament "exceed any rebuke of the Prophets of old."[28]

Loyd Gaston names this teaching found in Matthew the "displacement theory" and says that "beginning from the second century . . . the view that the church has supplanted Israel as the people of God . . . has been the greatest obstacle to the Christian understanding of Jews."[29] Douglas Hare says that this teaching has an even more ancient pedigree and that "Ruether is correct in claiming that the *Synoptic Gospels* . . . taught that the Jews had forfeited their place in God's plan of salvation and could no longer be regarded as his chosen people."[30] John T. Townsend calls this teaching "replacement theology,"[31] and while he might not disagree with Hare that "Matthew is particularly susceptible to such an interpretation,"[32] he notes that this theology is also found throughout the Gospel of John.[33] More particularly, in John, "Jesus has become the Law's replacement (cf. 1.17; 5.39f, etc.)."[34] He goes on to say that "in rabbinic circles, typical symbols for the Law of Moses included bread, light, water, and wine."[35] And in the Gospel of John, Jesus refers to himself as the "bread of life" (6.35-58), the "light of the world" (8.12), and "living water" (4.10).[36] Further, Townsend writes, "It is probable that John even has Jesus apply God's name to himself. In several instances, such as John 8.58 . . . Jesus uses the words [ἐγὼ εἰμί] ("I am") of himself without a predicate nominative. For Greek-speaking Jews and Christians those words could stand for the divine name,"[37] Townsend also says that "it is not surprising that Rosemary Ruether has found the fullest development of New Testament anti-Jewish bias within the *Gospel of John*," yet he believes "John's anti-Jewish bias generally appears to have entered the developing gospel at a relatively late stage."[38]

Some scholars (through the use of literary, source, form, and redaction criticism) question not only the authorship but the veracity of many (if not all) of the stories contained in the four canonical gospels. This presupposition, of course, leads to the questions surrounding the search for the "historical Jesus." In this interpretation, if most (if not all) of the texts of the four canonical gospels are discounted as pseudepigraphical, then there is no basis for any conclusions about the relationship of the mythological Jesus of Nazareth with the Jewish leaders. The importance of accepting this possibility is not inconsequential, for it speaks directly to the arguments of scholars who point to the New Testament as the source of all later Christian anti-Judaism and anti-Semitism. Also, accepting this possibility means that while the collection of books called the New Testament—finalized in the fourth century—contains stories and commentaries that portray the Jewish people of the first century in a very unflattering light, those views of the Jewish people cannot be placed at the feet of either Jesus (if, in fact, he did exist) or his Apostles Matthew, Mark, Luke, and John (if, in fact, they existed). Said in another way, the obvious anti-Judaism found in the canonical gospels are the inventions of later Christians, not the remembrances or inventions of the founders of Christianity, that is, Jesus and his Apostles.

There is one final comment before an analysis of the texts begins. While hundreds of thousands, if not millions of Christians over the past twenty centuries have used these texts to defame both Judaism and the Jewish people, neither anti-Judaism nor anti-Semitism are Christian inventions.[39] Jewish hatred is a global phenomenon that has existed for thousands of years.[40] Attempts have been made to understand this ongoing hatred, but none of the offered explanations are fully satisfactory.

As for Christian anti-Judaism, Gregory Baum, in his introductory remarks in Rosemary Ruether's book *Faith and Fratricide*, suggests that "anti-Jewish trends in Christianity are not simply peripheral and accidental, but woven into the core of the message."[41] Having concluded this to be so, he later asks whether removing the anti-Jewish virus destroys the Christian message.[42] In other words, can Christianity be Christianity without being anti-Jewish?

Shmuel Ettinger offers a number of theories, including the sociopsychological and the socioeconomic,[43] and while not discounting these, and even other theories, it is his exploration of the religious theories and his theory of intrinsic Anti-semitism that is the most intriguing. Under the subheading "Socioeconomic and Religious Theories," he writes:

> From the very start, Christianity appeared on the historical stage as a negation of Judaism and, when it attained power in affairs of State, it turned opposition to Judaism and oppression of the Jews into an official slogan. It pushed Jews to the margins of society, forcing them into economic activity and a social class that aroused their neighbor's hatred. There is no doubt that this argument has a good deal of truth to it despite that fact that Jew-hatred [both literary and popular] preceded the advent of Christianity. Not a few of the early Christians bore it with themselves as a result of their pagan upbringing.[44]

Under the subheading "Theory of Intrinsic Antisemitism," Ettinger explores a theory that is very akin to the "blaming the victim" exploration of oppressed people by the oppressors. He writes,

> We conclude with an additional explanation, one that is traditionally popular among antisemites who see the cause of antisemitism in the Jews themselves. So claimed Servatius, Eichmann's attorney during the [Nurnberg] trial; and Dostoevsky who, in his famous article on the Jewish question, asked: Why has everyone always hated the Jews? Can some general meaning be imputed to this phenomenon? After all, we are speaking of societies that have existed throughout history, from the Hellenistic era up to the present time. The peoples who persecuted the Jews had different social systems, cultures, and governments, yet common to all was their hatred of the Jews. The only possible explanation for this is that the cause of antisemitism is inherent in the Jews themselves: in their way of life, law, and deeds.[45]

I believe what Ettinger and the others are saying is that Christian anti-Judaism and anti-Semitism was not invented out of "whole cloth." It had precedents in the ancient world. Leon Sheleff reminds us that "there are many reasons for classical anti-Semitism—including the unfortunately ever-present phenomenon of xenophobia," but "the Crucifixion is undoubtedly of major importance, and it related directly to much of the essence of Christian theology."[46] Ettinger is also saying that the early Christians "Christianized" anti-Judaism and anti-Semitism with such effectiveness that when the cultures of the ancient and medieval world became Christian, the anti-Judaism and anti-Semitism that had become embedded in those earlier cultures were carried forward with them.

Therefore, some scholars, both Christian and Jewish, see anti-Judaism and anti-Semitism as an inherent part of Christian theology, and, as Ettinger has pointed out, some see anti-Semitism as inherent in the Jews. I would suggest that anti-Judaism and anti-Semitism, like all religious and racial bigotry, is inherent in humanity. However, I also believe that if that part of our essence cannot be totally eradicated, it can, at least, be recognized and kept in check. We cannot continue to repeat the sins of racial bigotry of our fathers and mothers who often read the conflicts between Jesus and the Jewish leaders as evidence that the Jewish people have always resisted God and His gifts of salvation and that they have continued to refuse stubbornly to accept the second person of the Christian Godhead. Townsend says that many of these Christians believe that the Jews "have no right to call themselves children of Abraham" and that "even though the Mosaic Law belongs to the Jews, they themselves have failed to understand it, for they have never known God."[47] This arrogant disownment of the Hebrew Tanakh for the Jewish people by Christians began in the first century and has continued to today. These Christians continue to believe that because of the Jews' "hard-heartedness," God has rejected the Jewish people and visited on them all manner of judgments. Many of these judgments are viewed as just recompense for the rejection of Jesus, and Christians should feel no compunction for being God's agents in meting out His judgments on the Jewish people. Meagher notes that Christians have "claimed to be the heirs of all that Judaism offered, and more . . . and that Judaism was quite obsolete.[48]

Although many in the 21st century would find this a horribly distorted expression of Christianity, Gaston quotes Ruether as saying, "Possibly anti-Judaism is too deeply embedded in the foundations of Christianity to be rooted out entirely without destroying the whole structure."[49]

Moving from the gospels to the epistles, Gaston wonders whether Paul "is able to proclaim his gospel of grace only against the dark foil of Jewish legalism," even though "the rabbis never speak of Torah as the means to salvation."[50]

Yet these beliefs and attitudes about the Jewish religion and Jewish people have led to the death of millions of innocent victims. It is a social problem, a theological problem, a spiritual problem, a cultural problem, a historical problem, and, in its most virulent form, it is a racial problem. *And it is a problem in which the Jewish people bear no responsibility.*

Donald A. Hagner has perhaps summed up the sentiment with which more Christians must wrestle

> There can be no question but that the Holocaust—that ripest and most bitter fruit of anti-Semitism—perpetrated by the leadership of an at least nominally Christian nation, constitutes a fundamental turning point in Jewish-Christian relations. It should no longer be possible for Christians to remain unaware of the evil that can be caused by an improper or insensitive use of the anti-Judaic statements of the New Testament. Christians from now on must be vigilant against every manifestation of anti-Semitism and every misuse of New Testament materials that leads to anti-Semitism. Because of the possibility of misunderstanding these texts, we have reached the point where it is now necessary for every exposition of the anti-Judaic passages of the New Testament to be accompanied by explicit statements concerning what they do *not* mean. Anti-Judaism is theological *disagreement* with Judaism, and . . . this disagreement can become polemical in tone. Anti-Semitism, by contrast, is nothing less than racial *hatred* of the Jews, a hatred that can take a variety of forms such as prejudice, injustice, slander, abuse, and even physical violence.[51]

However, in saying this, I am not condemning Christianity, nor am I prepared to fix blame on all Christians. I am writing this book to take as objective a look at early Christian anti-Judaism and anti-Semitism as is possible. And while it is tempting (and easy) to trace all attacks on Judaism and the Jewish people in the Common Era back to the beginning of Christianity, many of the later conflicts had more to do with racial bigotry, power, and money that were cloaked with charges of deicide.

Notes

1. All Scripture references are from the *New King James Bible* unless noted otherwise. Further, throughout the book, when referring to Jesus in the third person singular pronoun I will use an uppercase "H" (He, Him, His) to avoid confusion when referencing other males in the third person singular in the text.

2. David Rokeah, "The Church Fathers and the Jews in Writings Designed for Internal and External Use," in *Antisemitism through the Ages*, ed. Shmuel Almog (New York: Pergamon Press, 1988), 41.

3. Rosemary Ruether writes that the teachings of Jesus were "not entirely different . . . from that of the contemporary school of Hillel." Rosemary Ruether, *Faith and Fratricide: The Theological Roots of anti-Semitism* (Minneapolis, MN: Seabury Press, 1974), 66.

4. I have chosen to use the Hebrew word for the Jewish Holy Scriptures "Tanakh," the Hebrew acronym for *Torah* (Law or Pentateuch), *Nevi'im* (Prophets), and *K'tuvim* (Sacred Writings), throughout this book when referring to what Christians have commonly called the Old Testament.

5. The Hebrew word "Torah;" meaning law or teaching, was translated as νόμος by the third century BCE Jewish scholars who translated the Tanakh from Hebrew to Greek. And as Torah can be a reference to various laws in the Tanakh, so νόμος in the New Testament can be a reference not only to the Laws of Moses, but to the entire Tanakh.

6. The word translated "entangle" in the NKJV comes from the Greek word παγιδεύω, which Thayer says "is unknown to the Greeks." It literally means "to ensnare or entrap" and metaphorically it is used to speak of an "attempt to elicit from one some remark which can be turned into an accusation against him." Joseph Henry Thayer, trans. *A Greek-English Lexicon of the New Testament* (Grand Rapids, MI: Zondervan Publishing House, 1889), 472.

7. Much of what is called "The Sermon on the Mount" (Mt 5–7) is the best example of this.

8. It has been argued for quite some time, with some very convincing arguments, that the Apostle Paul is the founder of Christianity. However, whether one believes that the foundation of Christianity is the teachings and sacrifice of Jesus of Nazareth or the theology of the Apostle Paul, the teachings and sacrifice of the central figure in Christianity must be considered especially in a study of the foundations of Christian anti-Judaism and anti-Semitism. Early and modern examples of those who have or are participating in the argument are: Wm. H. Johnson, "Was Paul the Founder of Christianity?" *Princeton Theological Review* V (1907): 398–422; Robin Griffith-Jones, *The Gospel According to Paul: The Creative Genius Who Brought Jesus to the World* (New York: HarperSanFrancisco, 2004); Gerd Ludemann, *Paul: The Founder of Christianity* (Amherst, NY: Prometheus Books, 2002); David Wenham, *Paul, Follower of Jesus or Founder of Christianity* (Grand Rapids, MI: Wm. B. Eerdmans, 1995).

9. John C. Meagher, "As the Twig Was Bent: Antisemitism in Greco-Roman and Earliest Christian Times," in *AntiSemitism and the Foundations of Christianity*, ed. Alan T. Davies (New York: Paulist Press, 1979), 12–13.

10. Bruce Chilton, "Jesus and the Question of anti-Semitism," in *Anti-Semitism and Early Christianity: Issues of Polemic and Faith*, ed. Craig A. Evans and Donald A. Hagner (Minneapolis, MN: Fortress Press, 1993), 40.

11. Eduard Schweizer believes that the writer of the Gospel of Mark was also indebted to Q, and writes that Q was "first used by Mark, and then Matthew and Luke would have had both this prototype and the Gospel of Mark before them." Important studies on Q in English are: Marcus Borg, ed., *The Lost Gospel Q: The Original Sayings of Jesus* (Berkeley, CA: Ulysses Press, 1996); Arland Dean Jacobson, *The First Gospel: An Introduction to Q* (Sonoma, CA: Polebridge Press, 1991); John S. Kloppenborg, *The Formation of Q: Trajectories in Ancient Wisdom Collections* (Philadelphia, PA: Fortress Press, 1987); _____, *Q Parallels: Synopsis, Critical Notes, and Concordance* (Sonoma, CA: Polebridge Press, 1988); Burton Mack, *The Lost Gospel: The Book of Q and Christian Origins* (San Francisco, CA: Harper San Francisco, 1993); and Leif Vaage, *Galilean Upstarts: Jesus' First Followers According to Q* (Valley Forge, PA: Trinity Press International, 1994).

12. Bart D. Ehrman writes about the possibilities of redactors to the gospels of Matthew and Luke in his introduction to the New Testament. Bart D. Ehrman, *The New Testament: A Historical Introduction to the Early Christian Writings*, (New York: Oxford University Press, 2000), 76–82.

13. Marvin Perry and Frederick M. Schweitzer, *Antisemitism: Myth and Hate from Antiquity to the Present*, (New York: Palgrave MacMillan, 2002), 19. This seems to be taken from E. P. Sanders, "Jews and Judaism," *Theology Today* 51 (April 1995): 15.

14. Elaine Pagels and Karen L. King, *Reading Judas: The Gospel of Judas and the Shaping of Christianity* (New York: Viking Press, 2007), 6.

15. See figure 6.1 on p. 77 of Ehrman's book. Ehrman, *The New Testament*, 77.

16. It is doubtful that the Jewish leaders felt a need for forgiveness for saving their people from what they believed to be another charlatan.

17. Loyd Gaston, "Paul and the Torah," in *AntiSemitism and the Foundations of Christianity*, ed. Alan Davies (New York: Paulist Press, 1979), 48.

18. Ruether, *Faith and Fratricide*, 68, 69.

19. A thorough examination of the *adversus judaios* of the early Church Fathers appears in volume 2 of this study.

20. This view, however, must be tempered by the recognition of the more than few stories of conflict between Jesus and the religious leaders in the gospel of Mark

21. Claudia Setzer, *Jewish Reponses to Early Christians: History and Polemics, 30–150 C.E.*, (Minneapolis, MN: Fortress Press, 1994), 34.

22. Douglas R.A. Hare, "The Rejection of the Jews in the Synoptic Gospels and Acts," in *AntiSemitism and the Foundations of Christianity*, ed. Alan T. Davies (New York: Paulist Press, 1979), 29

23. Ruether, *Faith and Fratricide*, 65.

24. Chilton, "Jesus and the Question of anti-Semitism," 40.

25. Meagher, "As the Twig Was Bent," 19.

26. Scot McKnight, "A Loyal Critic: Matthew's Polemic with Judaism in Theological Perspective," in *Anti-Semitism and Early Christianity: Issues of Polemic and Faith*, ed. Craig A. Evans and Donald A. Hagner (Minneapolis, MN: Fortress Press, 1993), 56.

27. Ibid.

28. Ibid., n. e. See L. T. Johnson, " The New Testament's Anti-Jewish Slander and the Conventions of Ancient Polemic," *Journal of Biblical Literature* 108 (1989), 441. Also M. J. Cook, "Anti-Judaism in the New Testament," *Union Seminary Quarterly Review 38* (1983), 125–126.

29. Gaston, "Paul and the Torah," 51.

30. Hare, "The Rejection of the Jews in the Synoptic Gospels and Acts," 27.

31. John T. Townsend, "The Gospel of John and the Jews: The Story of a Religious Divorce," in *AntiSemitism and the Foundation of Christianity*, ed. Alan Davies (New York: Paulist Press, 1979), 72.

32. Hare, "The Rejection of the Jews in the Synoptic Gospels and Acts," 27.

33. Townsend, "The Gospel of John and the Jews," 72.

34. Ibid.

35. Ibid.

36. It is in the synoptics that Jesus, during the Passover meal, says that the wine is "My blood of the new covenant." (Mt. 26.26–29; Mk 14.22–25; Lk 22.19, 20).

37. Townsend, "The Gospel of John and the Jews," 74.

38. Ibid., 84.

39. See Meagher, "As the Twig is Bent, 1–25. The notes for this chapter of Davies book are very helpful in understanding the pre-Christian expressions of anti-Judaism and anti-Semitism in the ancient Greek and Roman world.

40. Excellent studies that speak to this issue are as follows: Rosemary Ruether, *Faith and Fratricide* (Minneapolis, MN: Seabury Press, 1974), 23–63; Menahem Stern, "Anti-semitism in Rome," in *Antisemitism Through the Ages*, ed. Shmuel Almog (New York: Pergamon Press, 1988), 13–25; Moshe David Herr, " The Sages' Reaction to Anti-semitism in the Hellenistic-Roman World," in *Antisemitism Through the Ages*, ed. Shmuel Almog (New York: Pergamon Press, 1988), 27–38; John C. Meagher, "As the Twig Was Bent: Antisemitism in Greco-Roman and Earliest Christian Times," in *AntiSemitism and the Foundations of Christianity*, ed. Alan T. Davies (New York: Paulist Press, 1979), 1–26; John G. Gager, *The Origins of Anti-Semitism: Attitudes Toward*

Judaism in Pagan and Christian Antiquity (New York: Oxford University Press, 1983), 39-115. Gager chooses to approach this subject from three different angles. Chapters 4, 5, and 6 are titled, "The Greek and Roman Encounter with Judaism *Phil-osophy and Politics*," "Against the Stream: Sympathy for Judaism in Imperial Rome," and "Roam Policy Toward Judaism and the Rise of Christianity."

41. Gregory Baum, Introduction to *Faith and Fratricide: The Theological Roots of Anti-Semitism*, by Rosemary Ruether (Minneapolis, MN: Seabury Press, 1974), 5. Ruether's conclusions, and her methodologies used to reach these conclusions have been discussed in other books. My intention here, is to list the major explanations for the admitted anti-Jewish history that is part of the legacy of the Christian church.

42. Ibid., 11.

43. Shmuel Ettinger, "Jew-Hatred in its Historical Context," in *Antisemitism through the Ages*, ed. Shmuel Almog (New York: Pergamon Press, 1988), 1–12.

44. Ibid., 8.

45. Ibid.

46. Leon Sheleff, *In the Shadow of the Cross: Jewish-Christian Relations Through the Ages* (Portland, OR: Vallentine Mitchell, 2004), 11.

47. Townsend, "The Gospel of John and the Jews," 72.

48. Meagher, "As the Twig was Bent," 23.

49. Gaston, "Paul and the Torah," 48.

50. Ibid., 49, 51.

51. Donald A. Hagner, "Paul's Quarrel with Judaism," in *Anti-Semitism and Early Christianity: Issues of Polemic and Faith*, ed. Craig A. Evans and Donald A. Hagner (Minneapolis, MN: Fortress Press, 1993, 128.

Chapter 1
Conflict in the Gospels

The "Son of Man" as the Messiah

There is little agreement as to the source(s) of the conflict between Jesus and the religious leaders, but I find myself agreeing with Rosemary Ruether, who writes that

> the crux of the conflict lay in the fact that the Church erected its messianic midrash into a *new principle of salvation*. For Christianity, salvation was now found . . . solely through faith in the messianic exegesis of the church about the salvific role of Jesus as Prophet—King—*Son of man*, predicted by the prophets.[1]

It is my contention that while there were differences between Jesus and the religious leaders over the function and interpretation of Torah, it was Jesus' constant claim to be the Messiah that continually caused the encounters and conflicts to erupt into verbal fights, which included threats of exile from the community and even death. Jesus of Nazareth, through His claims as the "Son of Man," was guilty of the worst kind of blasphemy. And although Jesus never specifically referred to Himself as the (or "a") long-promised Jewish Messiah, even a casual reading of the canonical Gospel texts reveals that He believed Himself to be that Messiah. The preferred term for Jesus for this self-declaration was the term "Son of Man," and an examination of the language used by Jesus to describe the attributes of the "Son of Man" to his disciples, to the religious leaders, and to the common people makes this clear.

Leon Sheleff argues that it is not unreasonable "that any such claim by Jesus to be the Son of God may well have led to a vicious response by the Jewish religious authorities."[2] However, this opinion is not unanimous, for Douglas Hare, along with others, believes that

> The Jewish community has always shown itself able to tolerate a wide variety of haggadic and halakic nonconformity within its midst, albeit with vigorous protest and healthy disagreement, [it was the] subordinating [of] all the primary symbols of Jewish identity—Torah, temple, circumcision, Sabbath, food laws—to a rank below the central Christian symbol of the crucified and risen Jesus [that the Jewish leaders viewed as] intolerable.[3]

In the end, it is very possible that, like many historical phenomena, there is no one reason for the conflict but a congregation of events and words that caused the end of Jesus to be what it was.

The Messiah in First Century Judaism

An important question, then, is "What did the Apostles, Jewish people, and especially the Jewish leaders hear when they heard Jesus refer to himself as the 'Son of Man?'" However, before that question can be answered, the question as to whether first century Jewish people even believed in a coming Messiah must first be addressed.

Joseph Klausner points out that the Hebrew word translated as "messiah" is associated with a number of personages in the Tanakh. He writes, "In the Holy Scriptures kings, Israelite [1 Sam 24.7] and foreign [Isa 45.1], and high priests [Lev 4.3] are described by this word, for all of these were anointed with oil . . . But other men also . . . are called by this name."[4] Further, the word occurs twice (Ps 105.15; 1 Chron 16.22) to signify the prophets, and in other places (Ps 89.39, 52; 84.10) this word "designates the whole people [of] Israel."[5] Klausner continues to argue, through an examination of the books of Amos, Hosea, Isaiah, Micah, Nahum, Zephaniah, Habakkuk, Jeremiah, Ezekiel, Obadiah, Psalms, Deutero-Isaiah, Haggai, Zechariah, Joel, Malachi, and Daniel, that the Messianic ideal "was not born at one moment, but developed during the course of several generations."[6] Klausner continues by saying that the "Jewish Messianic idea, in its authentic form, came forth from an essentially political aspiration . . . [and] the kingdom of the Jewish King-Messiah was and remained . . . a kingdom of this world."[7] Lillian Freudmann agrees and states that Jesus' declaration of himself as the Messiah "was not lost on the Romans. This was a political statement which the Romans understood only too well. It meant rebellion and treason."[8] Jacob Neusner writes that in the "pre-Christian and pre-rabbinic religion of Israel, for all its variety, [it] exhibited common traits of belief," including "the expectation of a coming Messiah to restore all the Jews to Israel and end the anguish of history."[9] Lillian Freudmann writes that the role of the Messiah was "manifold":

> He would free the Jews from oppression and their land from conquerors. He would inaugurate universal peace. Through him would come the recognition and worship by all mankind of the one God of Israel. He would be a harbinger of social justice throughout the world.[10]

Philip Alexander argues that "early Judaism did know of powerful semi-divine mediator figures"[11], and John C. Meagher writes,

> Many [ancient] scenarios envision a messiah who would lead the battle, or bring the subsequent peace into theocratic order, or, occasionally, merely preside decoratively over the resultant restoration. But other scenarios offer no messiah, only the cataclysmic intervention of God and his angels."[12]

However, while many will agree that there were expectations of a Messiah, they do not believe that the term "Son of Man" was ever, in the Hebrew, used in this manner. Sheleff argues that in Hebrew "the Son of Man is no more than a person."[13] He adds,

> The use in the New Testament of the phrase the "Son of Man" may likely have no real relevance, since the term is merely a common vernacular in Hebrew or other Semitic languages that posed problems in later translations.[14]

Sheleff supports his position by quoting C. H. Dodd who writes, "There is little evidence to show that in pre-Christian Judaism the term 'Son of Man' was used as a Messianic title."[15]

However, it is the literary evidence from contemporary and near contemporary Jewish (not Christian) sources, pointing to a widespread belief in a future Messiah that may be the most compelling.[16]

A) Jewish Apocrypha (ca. 1st–2nd BCE): In 2 Esdras 7.26–30 and 12.31–34, the text refers to either "my son the Messiah" or "the Messiah" three times. In these passages, this Messiah will bring a judgment and a seven-day cataclysm to the earth so devastating that it will destroy both Him and all living beings on earth. However, a remnant of His people He will be saved and set free.

B) Jewish Pseudepigrapha (ca. 2nd c. BCE–1st c. CE):

1) 1 Enoch 46.1ff; 48.2–20; 52.4; 62.5, 7, 14; 69.29; and 70.1: In these passages, the "Son of Man" is mentioned nine times and the passages in ch. 48 the "Chosen One" and "His Messiah" also seem to be referencing the "Son of Man." In these texts, the emphasis is on the Son of Man sitting on a throne of Glory passing judgment.

2) Psalms of Solomon: In ch.17.21–18.9, the "Messiah" is mentioned three times. The text says that "their king shall be the Lord Messiah,"

"the Messiah will reign," and the people will be "under the rod of discipline of the Lord Messiah."

3) 2 Baruch: In chs. 29.3; 30.1; 39.7; 40.1f; and 72.2, the "Anointed One" (Heb = "Messiah") is mentioned five times. In these passages, the "Anointed One" will, in the future, be revealed, and He will bring judgment with Him.

C) Dead Sea Scrolls (ca. 2nd c. BCE–1st c. CE): Three of the documents from the Dead Sea Scrolls, that is, CD (*Damascus Document*), 1QS (*The Rule of the Community*), and 4Q252 frag 1, Col 5 (on Gen 49.10), speak of either the "Messiah of Aaron" or the "Messiah of Aaron and Israel," or the "Messiah of justice . . . the branch of David." In these passages, the Messiah seems to be both a king and a savior.

D) Targumim (2nd Temple Era: 536 BCE–70 CE): Aramaic translations of the Tanakh where the term Messiah is used over 75 times in the Law, Prophets, History, and Wisdom Literature. The authors of the Christian Think Tank sum up its use in the Targumim.

> The Messiah will be the symbol and/or the active agent of the deliverance of Israel. He will be of Davidic lineage, though he may have a non-Davidic predecessor, the Ephraimite Messiah, who will die in battle. Elijah will herald his coming and will serve as His High Priest. A world conflict will rage between Rome, variously identified with Gog, Amalek, Edom, and Armilus, on the one hand, and Assyria or Eber, on the other, indicating that to the Targumist, Assyria and Babylon was the real enemy of Israel, and this will result in the annihilation of both at the time of the Messianic advent; the enemies of Israel will be shattered either by divine or Messianic intervention. The Messiah will bring an end to the wandering of Israel, and the Jewish people will be gathered in from their Dispersion to their own land; The Northern Kingdom will be reunited with Judah. The drama of the Exodus from Egypt will be re-enacted; in this drama Moses may participate, made possible by a resurrection of the dead. The Messiah will live eternally. He will restore the Temple and rebuild Jerusalem, which will enjoy divine protection for itself and its inhabitants. He will have sovereignty over all the world and make the Torah the universal law of mankind, with the ideal of education being realized to the full. The Messiah will have the gift of prophecy, and may have intercessory power to seek forgiveness of sin, but he will punish the unrepenting wicked of his people, as well as of the nations, and have the power to cast them into Gehenna. There will be a moral regeneration of Israel and of mankind. The Messiah will be a righteous judge, dispensing justice and equity, the champion of the poor and the oppressed, the personification of social justice. He will reward the righteous, who will surround him and eternally enjoy the divine effulgence. The essence of the Messiah will be faith in God; and he will vindicate that faith, and the faithfulness of Israel, in the eyes of all the world.[17]

E) Early Tannaic Writers: Although these were written post–New Testament, they are Jewish and not Christian, and there are passages in the

Mishnah, in both the Babylonian and Jerusalem Talmud, and in the Midrash numerous passages referencing the promise of the coming day of the Messiah.[18]

It can be concluded, then, with a fair degree of certainty that the concept of a coming Messiah was not unheard of in first century Palestine and that there were perhaps more than a few different beliefs of who the Messiah would be and what he would do when he appeared. B. M. Boksar writes that "Jews in the first two centuries [of the Common era] held diverse views" of the Messiah.[19] John Collins writes that in the Maccabean period (164–63 BCE), "there was no one 'orthodox' notion of the Messiah" and that the "presence or absence of messianism was primarily determined by the political attitudes and circumstances of the different groups within Judaism."[20] James Charlesworth concludes from his findings that

> We have numerous early Jewish sources that portray the Messiah variously, as one who will serve as the eschatological high priest (the Dead Sea Scrolls, the *T12P*), or as the consummate benevolent and all-powerful king (*PssSol 17*). Numerous functions are sometimes attributed to the Messiah: He will judge the wicked (*PssSol 17, 4 Ezra 12, 2 Bar 40*), destroy them (*PssSol 17, 4 Ezra 12, 2 Bar 72;* cf. Is 11), deliver God's people (*PssSol 17, 4 Ezra 12,* cf. Zech 9), and/or reign in a blessed kingdom (*PssSol 17, 18; 2 Bar 40;* cf. Ps 2).[21]

The canonical gospels represent first century Jewish writers (and with Luke, a non-Jewish writer) who believed that Jesus of Nazareth was the fulfillment of the promised Messiah, and E. Earle Ellis writes that these New Testament writers created a "thoroughgoing reinterpretation of the biblical writings to the person, ministry, death and resurrection of Jesus the Messiah."[22] And if he is correct in saying that "this messianic interpretation of scripture [was] understood as a break with Judaism" then this interpretation was not viewed as just another interpretation but a hostile appropriation of the Jewish sacred scriptures, for it negated traditional understandings of Jewish *Heils geschichte*. Jesus as the Messiah, as the "Son of Man," was the "fulfillment of that which was "prophesied the Old Testament."[23]

The "Son of Man" in the Q Gospel

The exact contents of the Q Gospel is not known, for no copy of it has survived (or been discovered to date), and because of the absence of a text, some assumptions have been made about the "Q community" based on what is believed to be in the Q Gospel. The belief of an absence of a Passion narrative in Q have led some to assume that in the Q communities, it was the teachings of Jesus rather than the sacrifice of Jesus that was of supreme importance. Of course, this assumption rests on the belief that there were, in fact Q communities, of which we have no evidence, and that in these Q communities, they were in possession of only a Q Gospel. If the dating of the Q Gospel is correct, these

Christians may have also been in possession of one or more of the letters of the Apostle Paul, in which the sacrifice of Jesus Christ is quite prominent.[24]

For the purposes of this study, according to the list found in Marcus Borg's study of the Q Gospel, there are only four references to the "Son of Man" (Mt 8.18–20; Mt 12.22–37; Mt 12. 38-45; and Lk 17.20–30).[25] M. A. Powell's list, found in David A. DeSilva's *Introduction to the New Testament*, adds a text from Matthew (Mt 11.2–19) and one from Luke (Lk 11.29–32; a parallel to the Mt 12.38–45 text) to the list compiled by Borg.[26] J. S. Kloppenborg also adds the text from Luke found in DeSilva's list.[27] This lack of agreement as to the con-tents of the Q Gospel is further complicated by the possibility that if the final texts of the four canonical gospels were the products of redactors, then it is also possible that the Q gospel was also redacted.

A more thorough analysis of these texts is found later in this chapter, but a quick look at these texts reveals some interesting things about how the compilers of the Q Gospel saw the "Son of Man."

Jesus as the "Son of Man" in the Mt 8 text makes no claims for Himself. He only says to a scribe that He is essentially homeless.

Mt 11.2–19 is the first of two Q passages in which Jesus, as the "Son of Man," speaks of "this generation."[28] After gently upbraiding John the Baptist's disciples and identifying John as the second coming of Elijah, Jesus turns His attention to "this generation," which He likens to children sitting in the marketplace complaining. The message here seems to be that John, who Jesus obviously admired, and He have both been condemned by these children sitting in the marketplace. John's restrictive diet caused some to say that he was demon possessed. The "Son of Man," however, "came eating and drinking" with tax collectors and sinners, and he earns the names of glutton and drunkard. What Jesus, or the creator of this story, has done here is identify Himself with the second coming of Elijah, a powerful prophet of God from earlier days, over against those who have condemned John and are condemning Jesus.

In Mt 12.22–37, after Jesus heals the demon-possessed man, the "multitudes" ask whether this could be "the Son of David?" It seems that the term "Son of David" was one of the ways of speaking of the Messiah in first century Palestine, for either the Pharisees (Mt 22.41–47) or the Scribes (Mk 12.35–37; Lk 20.41–44) or both are later questioned by Jesus about their belief that the Messiah is the "Son of David." So in this Q passage, the possibility is raised that Jesus is the Messiah by the common people as the "Son of David" and by Himself as the "Son of Man." Targum Jonathan on Jeremiah 30. 9, 21 reads, "And they shall worship before their God, and they shall hearken to Messiah, the Son of David, their King, whom I will raise up unto them."[29] But it is only after the religious leaders hear the question about Jesus being the Messiah that they charge Him with being in league with Beelzebub.

However, there are some scholars who question whether this even ever took place. Randal Helms writes, "This passage looks very much like an early Christian polemic, using a rather quibbling construction of a psalm to justify Jesus' messiahship despite his admitted lack of blood ties to David."[30]

The next Q passage that includes the "Son of Man" phrase is from Mt 12.38–45. The exact meaning of the word of Jesus here is open to some interpretation, but his argument goes something like this: Following his three days in the belly of a great fish, the pagan people of Nineveh repented at his preaching, and for that reason they will rise up in judgment and condemn "this generation." Likewise, the Queen of the South, (Sheba), a pagan queen, will also rise up in judgment and condemn "this generation," for she sought out the wisdom of Solomon. The implication here is that at the time of judgment, pagan individuals and even pagan nations, because they listened to messengers from God, will judge those who have not; even those who are part of the chosen people. And what is worse for this generation is that one greater than Jonah (a prophet from God} and Solomon (one of the great Kings of Israel) "is here." Therefore, if this is a passage from the Q gospel, a source for Matthew and Luke, it is evidence of an early belief in Jesus as a messenger from God that cannot be ignored without dire consequences. The liken passage reads, "For as Jonah became a sign to the Ninevites, so also the Son of Man will be to this generation" (11.30). The willingness of "this generation" to listen to the words of the "Son of Man" will determine whether they will give judgment or receive judgment.

The last Q passage to be considered here is from Lk 17.20–30. Answering a question posed to Him by some Pharisees about the arrival of the kingdom of God, Jesus speaks in vv. 22, 26 of the "days of the Son of Man" and vv. 24, 30 of the "day" of the "Son of Man." After telling them that the kingdom of God was "in their midst," he says three things about the day(s) of the "Son of Man."

A) v.22: At some point in the future, people will desire to see even one day of the "Son of Man," but it will be too late, for they "will not see it." This sounds like a day of judgment.

B) v.24: In His day, the "Son of Man" will be seen from one horizon to the next. If there was a belief that on a future day of judgment God would appear in the sky, this would bring that image to the minds of the people.

C) The judgment of water that fell on the earth in the days of Noah and the judgment of fire that fell on Sodom and Gomorrah in the days of Lot are types of the judgment that will fall in the future, for the people of the earth will have yet to give priority to spiritual matters, for there does not seem to be anything inherently wrong with eating, drinking, marrying, buying, selling, planting or building. Before that judgment comes, the "Son of Man" "must (Gr = δεῖ = it is necessary) suffer many things and be rejected by this generation," yet on that day of judgment the "Son of Man" will be revealed (v.30).

At least one conclusion, then, can be extrapolated from this information. It can be concluded that the compiler(s) of Q did see and were interested in Jesus as the Messiah and that His messianism was predominately expressed in the phrase "Son of Man."

The "Son of Man" in the Gnostic Writings

A full chapter will be devoted to early Christian Gnostic anti-Judaism in volume two of this series, but the inclusion of the occurrences of the phrase "Son of Man" in the Gnostic writings seems appropriate here. Surprisingly, of the various Gnostic Gospels, only the Gospel of Thomas (late 2nd ce.) and the Gospel of Philip (late 3rd ce.) use this term. In the Gospel of Thomas, it is another retelling of the story found in the Q Gospel and in Mt 8.18–22 and Lk 9.57–62, where Jesus says that the "Son of Man has no place to lay His head and rest."[31] It can be suggested, then, that because this story is found in four different early Christian sources, that this image of Jesus as the "Son of Man" was one that resonated with a number of His followers. But whereas the uses of the term "Son of Man" in the canonical gospels were often associated with conflict and strife, here it repeats a story of Jesus that demonstrates His unconcern with things material. If this can be considered a theological statement, it is one with which the Christian Gnostics would be comfortable.

In the Gospel of Philip, this phrase is found in two places separated by just a few verses. Its first occurrence in vv.75–76 is full of lacunae, and it is difficult to know what is being said about Jesus or even whether it is Jesus who is being referenced by the term. And while the portion of v.81 that carries the term "Son of Man" is intact, it still presents a philological knot difficult to untie. It reads, "There is the Son of Man and there is the son of the Son of Man. The Lord is the Son of Man, and the son of the Son Man is he who creates through the Son of Man. The Son of man received from God the capacity to create."[32]

Here the "Son of Man" is somehow associated with creation, and if it can be assumed that Gnostic believers attempted to be consistent in their theology, then the "Son of Man" is somehow associated with the very thing Gnostics saw as evil/carnal, that is things.[33]

There is, then, nothing in these two texts to suggest that the Gnostic believers were somehow anti-Judaic. Other Gnostic texts that use the term Son of Man" are *The Sophia of Jesus Christ* (late 1st ce.; 103–104, 105, 106, 108, 117–118),[34] *Eugnostics* (late 1st ce.; 81, 84),[35] *The Apocryphon of James* (early 2nd ce.; 1.3),[36] *The Dialogue of the Saviour* (early 2nd ce.; 135.37, 136.40),[37] *The Prayer of the Apostle Paul* (late 2nd ce.; 1.A.1),38 *The Treatise on the Resurrection* (late 2nd ce.; 44, 46),[39] *The Testimony of Truth* (late 2nd ce.; 30, 31, 32, 32, 36, 37, 37-38, 40, 40-41, 60, 61, 67, 69, 70-71, 72),[40] *The Apocalypse of Peter* (3rd ce.),[41] and *The Second Treatise of the Great Seth* (64, 65).[42]

In almost all of these texts, the author(s) attempt to identify who the Son of Man is. He is referred variously as "Son of God" (*Soph. Jes.* 105), "First Begetter" and "Saviour" (*Soph. Jes.* 108), the "Spirit, the Paraclete of [truth]" (*Pr. Paul* 1.A.1), "Son of God, Rheginos" (*Treat. Res.* 44), and "Jesus Christ" (*Treat. Seth* 65). This is not unusual, for the catholic Christians also adopted many names for Jesus that highlighted some aspect of either His person or His work.

The only text in the Gnostic corpus, however, where an attack on the Jews is coupled with the name "Son of Man" is found in *The Second Treatise of the Great Seth* 64. It reads, "[The Jews] never knew the truth, nor will they know it. For there is a great deception upon their soul, making it impossible for them to ever find a Nous (philosophy) of freedom in order to know him, until they come to know the Son of Man."

The point that needs to be made here is that while catholic Christians also accused the Jewish people of intellectual and/or spiritual incompetence, it can be argued that it was the charge of deicide that caused the most antipathy. That charge is not heard here because the Gnostic believers did not believe the Λόγος possessed a body and therefore could not be crucified. In fact, it was Simon of Cyrene who was crucified, not the Son of Man. Further, working from a belief that all good things, including salvation, comes from true γνῶσις, it not surprising that the author of this Gnostic text's main complaint against the Jewish people is that they never have and never will know the truth and the freedom that comes from philosophy only comes through a knowledge of the Son of Man. The purpose of the incarnation is revealed truth and not death on a cross.

However, Jewish people of the first few centuries of the common era, especially outside of Palestine, did not demonstrate a great antipathy toward philosophy, and Philo's work on the Tanakh reveals a reliability on philosophical concepts in his interpretations. It was perhaps the more common charge that the Jews were "enemies of mankind" that allowed divergent groups, religious and otherwise, to find in the Jewish people and the Jewish religion objectionable traits, that bled into all parts of their persona.

The "Son of Man" as Jesus' Most Common Self-identifying Term[43]

I will demonstrate that it was Jesus' self-identifying use of the term "Son of Man" (ὁ υἱὸς τοῦ ἀνθρώπου) that precipitously heightened the level of conflict between Jesus and the Jewish leaders.[44] Further, an examination of the context of its use supports this thesis. It is a term that we hear Jesus use in both the synoptics and in John, and it is a term that He used in the hearing of the following groups.[45]

A) Disciples: It can be assumed that the disciples were with Jesus at most of His self-declarations as the "Son of Man." However, Jesus uses this term when He is alone with some or all of his disciples in the following texts: Jhn 1.47–51; Mt 13.36–43; Mt 16.13–17; Mt 16.27–28; Mt 17.1–13 (Mk 9.2–9; Lk 9.28–36); Mt 19.27–30 (Mk 10.28–30; Lk 18.28–30); Mt 20.17–19 (Mk 8.31; Lk 9.20–22); Mt 20.25–28; and Jhn 13.31–35.

B) Religious leaders: The religious leaders heard Jesus use this term in the following texts: Mt 9.2-6 (Mk 2.1–10); Mt 12.38–45 (Lk 11.30); Lk 22.69; Lk 17.20–30: Lk 18.1–8; Lk 19.10; and Mt 26.57–68 (Mk 14.53–65; Lk 22.66–

71). Of these, only two are believed to be Q parallels; Mt 12.38–45 (Lk 11.30) and Lk 17.20–30.

C) General populace: Mt 11.7–19; Lk 19.1–10; Jhn 12.23; and Jhn 12.32–34.[46]

D) Mixed (disciples and/or religious leaders and/or general populace): Mt 9.2–6 (Mk 2.1–7; Lk 5.17–21); Jhn 5.19–47; Mt 12.1–8 (Mk 2.23–28; Lk 6.1–5); Mt 12.22–37 (Mk 3.22–27; Lk 11.17–23); Jhn 6.26–71; Jhn 8.12–59; Jhn 9.14–41; and Jhn 12.23–36.

E) Private audience: Jhn 3.11–21; and Mt 8.18–20 (Lk 9.57–62).

We can see, then, from these texts that Jesus began naming Himself as the "Son of Man" from the very beginning of His public ministry (Jhn 1.51) and continued to use the phrase to the very end (Mt 26.64). We begin with John 1.

The "Son of Man" in the Canonical Gospels

Jhn 1.47–51: The words of Jesus at the beginning of the Gospel of John, that the disciples, as His followers, will see the heavens open, and the angels of God will ascend and descend "upon the Son of Man" employ the same language used to describe the dream of Jacob in Gen 28.12, where he saw "a ladder set up on the earth, and its top reached to heaven; and there the angels of God were ascending and descending on it." In both the Genesis and gospel passage, it is "angels of God" ascending and descending, and the topmost reaches of the ladder are in heaven. It seems that, here, at the very beginning of His ministry, Jesus is unmistakenly announcing Himself to be either a messenger from God or a conduit to God—or both. As to whether the disciples recognized the parallels between the words of Jesus and the story in Genesis 28 and comprehended His words as ones which identified him as the conduit to is not told. In the dialogue between Jesus, Philip and Nathaniel, Jesus is identified in the following ways:

A) v.45: "Him of whom Moses in the law, and also the prophets wrote."—Philip

B) v.45: "the son of Joseph."—Philip

C) v.49: "the Son of God."—Nathanael

D) v.49: "the King of Israel."—Nathanael

E) v.51: "the Son of Man."—Jesus

It can, of course, be argued that Jesus' self-declaration of Himself as the "Son of Man" in v.51 has no relation to Him being declared as "Him of whom Moses and the law, and also the prophets wrote," or "the Son of God," or "the King of Israel." It was, after all, only He and not the disciples who named Him the "Son of Man" and that the disciples only saw Him as "Him of whom Moses in the law, and also the prophets wrote," and "the Son of God," and the King of Israel," but not the "Son of Man." However, if that is the case, then the final author of John would not have bothered to keep it in the text.[47]

Therefore, whether this encounter between Jesus and two of his early disciples is a faithful retelling of an event in the life of Jesus Christ or the work of a later redactor, Jesus is portrayed as a divine messenger and leader and one who has some sort of relationship with both the angels of heaven and heaven itself, unlike others of the chosen race. Therefore, even though he is the son of Joseph, he is also the "Son of God," and the "Son of Man." As the "King of Israel," he possesses not only spiritual power but political power as well.

Although the reaction of the disciples to the words of Jesus are not recorded, it can be assumed that if this conversation had taken place in the hearing of the political and spiritual leaders of Israel, the culmination of the still-to-come conflict between Jesus and his opposition may have lasted much less than three years.

Jhn 3.11-21: Jesus' use of the term "Son of Man in Jhn 3.13, 14 is, along with a passage in Mt 8, used in a context absent of conflict. However, His words here give the reader of this gospel an early view of who Jesus believed Himself to be. Verses 13–18 read,

> No one has ascended to heaven but He who came down from heaven, that is, the Son of Man.[48] And as Moses lifted up the serpent in the wilderness, even so must the Son of Man be lifted up, that whoever believes in Him should not perish but have eternal life. For God so loved the world that He gave His only begotten Son, that whoever believes in Him should not perish but have everlasting life. For God did not send His Son into the world to condemn the world, but that the world through Him might be saved. He who believes in Him is not condemned; but he who does not believe is condemned already, because he has not believed in the name of the only begotten Son of God.

If we can work past the theological accouterments that Christians (especially modern evangelical Christians) have added to these verses, which have made the words of Jesus almost cliché, we can find some important early understandings of who Jesus was thought to be. The thrust of this passage is clearly soteriological. The "Son of Man" has been sent by God (v.17) from heaven (v.13) to save the world (v.17), give eternal life to those who believe in Him (vv.16, 18), and as the snake-bitten Israelites on the plains of Edom were cured by looking upon the bronze serpent God instructed Moses to erect (see Num 21.1–9), so the "Son of Man" will be lifted up to save His people. Further, this passage reveals that Jesus believes Himself to be not only the "Son of God" (v.18) but the "only begotten Son" of God (vv.16, 18). It seems, then, that Jesus sees Himself as a son of God in a way unlike other Israeli men saw themselves as sons of God. He is the "only begotten Son" of God.

John does not reveal Nicodemus' reaction to the words of Jesus, but clearly Jesus uses language here that indicates that He has come to do a work for God which only He can do. Further, if He is the "only begotten Son of God" (τοῦ μονογενοῦς υἱοῦ τοῦ θεοῦ), then is He, the "Son of Man," also divine? A positive answer to this question would be either blasphemous or heretical to most (if not all) first century Jewish people, both Palestinian and Diasporic. Did Nicodemus, as a member of the political/religious oligarchy of Judea (the Sanhedrin) share these words with his fellow leaders? That question is not answered, but further encounters of Jesus and the religious leaders left them with no doubts to His claims to divine status.

Mt 8.18–20 (cf. Lk 9.57–62): In Mt 8, Jesus tells a "certain scribe" (in Luke "someone") and "another of his disciples" (in Luke, "another") that if they choose to follow Him, they must be prepared to sacrifice both creature and familial comforts. One of the ways of reading these texts is to conclude that this was Matthew's and Luke's (from Q?) way of reminding the readers and hearers of his gospel that the ascetic life that Jesus led was the model for the life Jesus expected His followers to lead. However, that Matthew would include a scribe as expressing interest in becoming a follower of Jesus, and that scribe addressing Jesus as "teacher" (rabbi) is of some interest. There is even a suggestion that this scribe is already a follower of Jesus, for v.21 speaks of "another of His disciples," implying that the scribe is also a disciple. However, while the other disciple is told to "follow me," the scribe is simply warned about the rigors of becoming a disciple of Jesus. The scribe does not receive the invitation the other disciple receives.

Mt 9.2–6 (cf. Mk 2.1–7; Lk 5.17–21): The ire of the religious leaders in this passage is raised because Jesus claims what is to them a divine prerogative by saying to the paralytic, "Son, be of good cheer; your sins are forgiven you." And when the religious leaders charge Jesus with blasphemy, He declares that "Son of Man's" ability to heal the man of his lameness is evidence enough of His right and authority to grant forgiveness from sin. Jesus does not require the man to go to the Temple to offer ritual sacrifices before the priests for his sins. The man is forgiven there in the home of a private citizen. The religious leaders quite naturally consider this an affront to much that is traditionally holy in Judaism; God, the Temple, and the divinely appointed mediators of God's forgiveness. This was to them clear evidence of blasphemy, which was by law in Israel punishable by stoning.[49]

Both Jerome and John Chrysostom, neither of whom could ever be mistaken for a supporter of Judaism, dismiss the charges of blasphemy against Jesus by the religious leaders, not because the charges are honest reactions to claims by an unknown teacher, but because of poisonous motives. Jerome says the scribes accused Jesus of blasphemy because they were "judgmental in construing the words of God."[50] Chrysostom dismisses the accusations of the religious leaders for "those who are malicious and all too full of themselves are always plotting against the good work of others."[51] We will discover, not surprisingly, through the analysis of other gospel passages that the early Fathers were always ready to read the darkest motives behind the reactions of the Jewish leaders to the words and works of Jesus.

Jhn 5.19–47: Although Jesus does not refer to Himself as the "Son of Man" until v.27, His references to the identity of the "Son of God" (v.25), and the spiritual intimacy between a father and his son, are articulated in such a way as to leave no mistake to His hearers that the "Father" is Jehovah and the "Son" is Jesus. That the Jewish leaders also understood Jesus' words this way is revealed in v.18: "Therefore, the Jews sought all the more to kill Him, because He not only broke the Sabbath, but also said that God was His Father, making Himself equal with God."[52] Therefore, it can be assumed that any further references in this passage to the "Father" and the "Son" would be understood by the Jewish leaders as references to God the Father and God's Son.

Verse 17 reads, "My Father has been working until now, and I have been working." This seems to be a theological justification for Jesus to heal people on the Sabbath, for in that work He is doing the same work as the Father. This same theme is repeated in vv.19–20, where Jesus says that all that He does is modeled after what He sees the Father do. However, not only are the healings of Jesus modeled after what the Father has shown Him, but greater work will be revealed; "For as the Father raises the dead and gives life to them, even so the Son gives life to whom He will." It can be assumed that most Jewish believers believed that only God had power over life and death, power to give life, and power to bring back to life. Therefore, any person who would publicly claim to have these powers, and to share them with God, would certainly be accused of blasphemy. Some views of the Messiah might include these powers, especially in the time of judgment, but for an unknown, itinerant preacher to claim these powers was intolerable.

It is in the time of judgment, according to this passage, that the ultimate fate of all who refuse to acknowledge that Jesus is the Christ will come to pass. All "judgment" has been given to the Son (v.22), and, at that time, equal "honor" (v.23) will be given to the Father and the Son. And only those who both hear and believe the voice of the Son will either escape judgment or be resurrected. Further, the reason Jesus has the power of judgment and power over life and death is because He is, within Himself, self-authenticating. All of this, He says, is "because He is the Son of Man" (v.27). The fate of all humanity, both good and evil, is in the hands of Jesus (vv.28–29).

Jesus then turns His attention, specifically, to the fate of the Jewish leaders, or as John repeatedly calls them, "the Jews." Townsend argues that evidence of John's "anti-Jewish bias," and "his negative portrayal of the Jewish people" is revealed through his repeated use of the terms "Jew" and "the Jews."[53] Townsend writes that while the other canonical gospel writers use these terms only five or six times, John uses them seventy-one times, and the cumulative "effect of this usage upon the reader is the implication that the Jews as a whole and not just the Jewish leaders were the enemies of Jesus."[54] Further, he notes that "the Jews in John appear so evil that some exegetes believe them to be not simply Jews, but a symbol for the evil hostility of the world to God's revelation."[55]

The reason they will charge Jesus with the crimes of blasphemy is because they refused to listen to the voices of witness that God sent—which range from John the Baptist (v.33), to the works of Jesus (v.36), and, perhaps the most inflammatory, both the Scriptures (v.39) and Moses (vv.45–47). For this reason Jesus says of them, "You have neither heard [God's] voice at any time, nor seen His form."

It would not be surprising if the reaction of the Jewish leaders to these words of Jesus ranged from contempt to horror. Jesus has, in effect, in this passage, nullified what they believed to be the bases and foundations of their religious and spiritual existence. God, God's holy word, and the believed author of Torah, Moses, have all been removed as references for understanding and truth, because these contemporary Jewish leaders refuse to believe in and listen to the words of Jesus of Nazareth. Townsend says that "For John, Jesus is a challenge to all the essential elements of the Jewish religion."[56] They are being asked to abandon all that they have believed and taught for hundreds of years and trust in a man who has just accused them of spiritual and theological malfeasance.

What makes this passage difficult for modern, Christian commentators is the degree of vitriol this early in the gospel. In other words, there are, in the Gospel of John, later stories of conflict between Jesus and the Jewish leaders that are far less antagonistic.[57] Is this confrontation, therefore, a later interpolation? Is this an actual story that John chose to put here instead of when it may have actually taken place? Or is this a story of a conflict that, as it progressed, became more antagonistic than it was ever intended to be? If this is a faithful rendering of an actual event in the life of Jesus, then it is one in which Jesus clearly reveals who He believes Himself to be, not in the private hearing of His disciples, but in the hearing of those who were to become His most ardent enemies. If, however, this is a later interpolation, then it is quite possible that the words put into the mouth of Jesus do not reflect His own self-understanding, or, perhaps more importantly, His apparent dismissing of the contemporary Jewish leadership.

Jhn 6.26–71: It is a commonly held axiom that the books of the Bible were not written in chapters, and John gives no evidence that the events in ch.6 were chronologically removed from the events of ch.5. In ch.5, the reader is told that Jesus' self-description of Himself as the judge of all humanity and the final arbiter over life, death, and resurrection, led the Jewish leaders toward persecution and they "sought to kill Him." Jesus was seen as a blasphemer of the worst kind. In ch.6, Jesus continues His assault on the Jewish belief on a reliance on anything or anyone other than God, by placing Himself as the hope for deliverance and eternal life.[58]

In language that is both mystical and metaphysical, Jesus says to those who followed Him to Capernaum (after He fed the 5,000) that they should "not labor for the food which perishes, but for food which endures to everlasting life, which the Son of Man will give you, because God the Father has set His seal on Him." Whatever that "food which endures" is, it brings everlasting life. Therefore, while there may have been some who believed Jesus was using "food" as a metaphor for "truth," Jesus makes it clear later that the food which brings everlasting life is His flesh and blood which true believers must eat and drink. In language that not even his disciples fully understood ("This is a hard saying; who can understand it?") Jesus almost dismisses the manna given to Israelites in the wilderness, for "the bread of God is He who comes down from heaven and gives life to the world." And when the people asked Jesus for this bread, He replied, "I am the bread of life," and in v.41, "I am the bread which came down from heaven."

Remembering that this conversation began with Jesus speaking of Himself as the "Son of Man," he says in v.37 that "the one who comes to Me I will by no means cast out." In v.39, Jesus says He will raise up "at the last day" all that the "Father sent Me." In v.40, He says "everyone who sees the Son and believes in Him [will] have everlasting life, and I will raise him up at the last day." Therefore, as in ch.5, Jesus is claiming divine prerogatives, and because some knew Jesus' mother (Mary) and father (Joseph), they "murmured against Him." He was, after all, a carpenter's son, and nothing they had either read or been taught mentioned a divine deliverer (the Messiah?) being the son of a carpenter from Nazareth. Jesus seems not to be dissuaded by the questions of His hearers, for He says again that in the last day He will raise up all that the Father sends to Him. In v.46, Jesus pushes their credulity even further by claiming that no one has seen the Father except Him.[59] Jesus is therefore even placing himself above Moses if His hearers remembered that Moses "hid his face" in the presence of God on Mt. Horeb for "he was afraid to look upon Him" (see Ex 6.3).

However, vv.48–58 are the most difficult of Jesus' words for His hearers to understand. He speaks of eternal life coming only to those who eat His flesh and drink His blood. His use of the words "unless" and "most assuredly" gives his statements a quality that they might not have otherwise. These statements caused the people to quarrel or argue with each other, and in the middle of their quarreling, Jesus says, "Most assuredly, I say to you, unless you eat the flesh of the Son of Man, and drink His blood, you have no life in you." Therefore, just as the "Son of Man" has a mystical union with His divine Father (Jehovah), so those who wish to have eternal life must enter into a mystical union with the "Son of Man."

In Jhn 5 and 6, then, Jesus, in language that is unmistakable, links Himself with God in ways that can only bring accusations of heresy, blasphemy, and even madness. He was seen as self-delusional, and He was guilty of the most extreme form of hubris. And if there were any who were still unconvinced that Jesus believed Himself to be divine, in Jhn 8.58 Jesus says, "Before Abraham was, I AM."

Mt 11.7–19 (cf. Lk 7.31–35): Jesus makes no claims for the "Son of Man" in this text but complains to the general populous that they have misjudged both Him and John the Baptist based either on their eating habits and/or their companions. He says that John was accused of having a demon because of his peculiar diet, but Jesus eats and drinks wine and is accused of being a glutton and a "winebibber" (Gr = οἰνοπότης; lit = wine-drinking). This is a rather strange accusation. Jesus was generally considered to be a teacher or rabbi, and as such would have had no injunctions in the Torah against drinking wine. Even if he were considered a prophet, there were still no rules against drinking wine. We have no record of Jesus misusing or abusing either food or wine. Even if the people had already accepted Him as a divine "Son of Man" there are simply no texts forbidding the coming Messiah to drink wine.

The wider context of this particular passage (ch.11) speaks of Jesus' frustration with the people for their inability to truly see spiritual things that are right before them. In other words, if they were truly spiritual people, they would certainly see that He was sent from God, not just to do miracles among them, but to also warn them of impending judgment. Contemporary pagan cities (Tyre and Sidon) and ancient cities (Sodom and Gomorrah) that received the fiery wrath of God will fare better in the judgment. Later in vv.25-27, Jesus speaks of the "Father, Lord of heaven and earth," as delivering all things to His Son. And so that no one misunderstands who the Son is, He says in v.27, "All things have been delivered to Me by My Father" and no one knows the Father "except the Son."

Mt 12.1–8 (cf. Mk 2.23–28; Lk 6.1–5): As the canonical Gospels are read, it becomes apparent that proper Sabbath observance, including "Sabbath rest," was exceedingly important to first century Palestinian Jewish people. They believed that the Sabbath, given to them by God, was memorialized in the Decalogue, written by the finger of God, and placed in the Ark of the Covenant, in the Most Holy Place in the Temple. Therefore, proper Sabbath observance was a sign of both ones allegiance to God and theological orthodoxy. Apparently, plucking grain and healing on the Sabbath were seen as violations of the Sabbath, and in Mt 8.1–13 Jesus and His disciples were guilty of both. Some Pharisees confronted Jesus about this and Jesus, in turn, reminds them that the Sabbath activities of the Temple priests are carried out without blame. In the holiest place, on the holiest day, anointed priests handle holy objects and are blameless. It is difficult to imagine anything more sacred for first century Jewish people than being in the holy Temple on the holy day. The Pharisees would understand this, and then Jesus says to them that He, the "Son of Man," is greater than the Temple, and that He is greater than the Sabbath, for He is the Lord "even of the Sabbath." The Temple was the traditional dwelling place of God; the place where God manifested His glory.[60] Therefore, a person claiming that He is greater than the holy Temple, and that He is the Lord of the holy Sabbath is clearly claiming divine status. Early Christians hearing these words of Jesus would hear him claiming his rightful status, but the Pharisees obviously could not accept this and would have to accuse Jesus of both unmitigated hubris and rank blasphemy.

Mt 12.22–37: In this passage, the multitudes are again amazed and wonder out loud whether Jesus could be the long-looked for "Son of David" (v.23), elevating him to a status far beyond any of the present population, including the present-day religious leaders.[61]

As before, however, the approbation for Jesus was not unanimous, and it seems that the religious leader's main concern was not what Jesus was doing but how he was being perceived by the crowds.

The Pharisees respond not so much to Jesus' exorcism as to the crowds. The narrative accordingly implies that what the Pharisees are interested in above all is keeping others from belief. . . . The Pharisees, we may observe, refer to Jesus not in the second person, but in the third person. They are not arguing with the healer, but with the onlookers.[62]

One ancient commentator writes that the Pharisees "were roused to jealousy" and "attempted to prevent people from believing in Jesus after seeing his miracle."[63]

Perhaps the most troubling (or revealing?) part of this passage are the words of Jesus in v.34, "How can you, being evil, speak good things?" Just as the Pharisees attempted to place Jesus in league with a known evil entity (Beelzebub), Jesus says that the only presence of evil there resided in the persons of the Pharisees. However, it is not an evil that is unforgivable, for in v.32 Jesus says, "Anyone who speaks a word against the Son of Man, it will be forgiven him; but the blasphemy against the Spirit will not be forgiven men."

What we have here, then, in these two pericopes from Mt 12, are stories that illustrate attempts by the religious leaders of Israel to convince the people of Israel of the invalidity of the work of Jesus. If they can convince the multitudes that the power of Jesus comes, not from God, but from Satan (read: Beelzebub), Jesus will be seen as another charlatan who has no standing either with God or with the established religious leadership, and therefore, with the crowd. Whether they were concerned about the people being led astray or whether they were concerned about losing authority over the people (or both) depends on one's belief in the motives of the religious leaders. Augustine, echoing the belief of many of the early Church Fathers implies that the religious leaders had aligned themselves with Satan.

> Let the Pharisees choose what they want. If Satan could not cast out Satan, they could find nothing to say against the Lord. But if Satan can cast out Satan, let them look out for themselves all the more and let them abandon his kingdom because it cannot stand divided against itself.[64]

Although, historically, Christians have followed Augustine's lead and attributed less savory motives to the Pharisees, it was not necessary, in the succeeding centuries, to continue to rehearse these old beliefs about the Jewish religious leaders.

It is difficult to understand the response of Jesus, in Mt 12.38–39 (cf. Lk 11.29) to the request of the scribes and Pharisees to demonstrate to them, by some commonly recognized sign that his work originates from God. This request from the scribes and Pharisees may have become part of a standard battery of tests and questions that the religious leaders asked all those who were claiming to be either the Messiah or a messenger from God. It is an accepted axiom that Jesus was not the only independent, non-recognized preacher/teacher roaming Israel in the first century C.E. Understood in this context, the request of the scribes and Pharisees is seen as an attempt to discover who he was, not as an attempt to unveil Jesus as an untrained, uneducated religious zealot, who could be easily be embarrassed.

However, either Jesus, or Matthew, or the author of this story sees the request of the scribes and Pharisees as unreasonable, and Jesus' response is the response of a man who had concluded that the request was not coming from an honest desire for truth. Therefore, Jesus does not give to these religious leaders any answer that they can use against him but rather one that was unexpected.

In conclusion, this exchange cannot be used as a justification by later Christians to condemn all of the Jewish people of Jesus' day, nor certainly the Jewish people of later generations, for he is only addressing those from this present "generation" who are seeking a sign.

As in this text, scribes, Pharisees, Sadducees, priests, and the chief priest, sometimes alone, and sometimes in tandem, appear in many stories in the gospels as the protagonists of Jesus and his disciples. Whether the stories are accurate as to exactly who it was who was confronting Jesus is not as important, as the desired perception that most of the Jewish religious leaders in and around Judea are unsympathetic to Jesus and his followers.

The early Christians and Jewish people who either read or heard this story would react in at least two ways. For some of the Jewish faithful, their doubts about Jesus as the Jewish Messiah would be confirmed, for not only are He and His followers openly discounting long-held, sacred, Jewish traditions, but He is saying that these traditions do not come from God, but from men, and as such, are of no value.[65] Further, in this story, Jesus does not deny that His followers are transgressing the "tradition[s] of the elders." All faithful Jewish believers know that transgression of traditions taught by the "elders" (religious leaders) brought retribution either from the rest of the Jewish community or possibly from God. Yet Jesus does not seem to be concerned about this. Instead He accuses the scribes and Pharisees of even greater spiritual crimes. Jesus accuses them of transgressing, not traditions, but the commandments of God, and it is their traditions that are the cause for this even greater transgression. Further, the scribes and Pharisees have caused the commandments of God to be of no effect in the lives of the people. Jesus quotes Isaiah 29.13 to charge these present day religious leaders with hypocrisy, giving the appearance of faithfulness to God; but it is appearance only. Jesus ups the ante by telling the scribes and Pharisees, and everyone else in the crowd, that their (the scribes and Pharisees) worship of God is worthless because it is based on traditions ("the teachings of men") rather then the teachings of God. In effect, Jesus is saying that the traditions that the people are being taught either are not based on the teachings of God or are incorrect understandings of the teachings of God. In either case, they are not just harmless but absolutely, spiritually harmful.

Matthew does not record any response from the scribes and Pharisees, but it can be assumed that they would argue that their traditions concerning Sabbath keeping, dietary restrictions, and the rest are faithful interpretations of the word and will of God, and it is these teachings and traditions that they pass along to the present and future generations that keeps the knowledge of God's purpose and design for his people alive. However, when Hare writes that later Christian Jews, "by subordinating all the primary symbols of Jewish identity—Torah, temple, circumcision, Sabbath, food laws—to a rank below the central Christian symbol of the crucified and risen Jesus" and that these teachings "challenged ethnic solidarity too severely to be tolerated," he attempts to hear what these first century Jewish leaders heard.[66] Setzer argues that the Jewish charges against the teachings of the post-crucifixion apostles of "blasphemy, speaking against the Temple, speaking against the Law, and changing Mosaic customs," arose out of the apostles "proclaiming Jesus resurrection and teaching in Jesus name."[67] If we can assume that the scribes and Pharisees would defend their teachings, based on their traditions, what we have then becomes a question of competing hermeneutic. In this text, Jesus is not allowing the religious leader's interpretation of God's will as another equally valuable interpretation to his own. Not only is it dismissed, but it is dangerous. It seems that Jesus is not content to let the teachings of the religious leaders continue unchallenged, and it is perhaps here in the gospels, for the first time, that the reader can begin to comprehend the profound theological change that Jesus is demanding. If it is true that a great deal of Jewish religious identity arises from what are believed to be correct interpretations of the Torah, then a challenge of this magnitude must, by the Jewish leaders, be rejected. They cannot allow this unlearned teacher to charge them with spiritual and theological turpitude.

Finally, when Jesus gets his disciples alone, responding to their fears that Jesus is offending the leaders, he tells them to ignore the scribes and Pharisees, for they are blind.

It appears from this story that it is the perceived perversion of the teachings of God that causes Jesus to lash out at the scribes and Pharisees. The magnitude of the words of Jesus here can hardly be overstated. Jesus appears to be saying that the Jewish leaders are guilty of bringing God's chosen people to a place of national disobedience of God, and the guilt is especially egregious because the leaders are masking their "commandments of men" as the doctrines of God. Therefore, if the Jewish people continue to follow these blind guides, their own blindness will not be apparent until it is too late.

However, it must also be remembered that the religious leaders of Israel were engaged in the same enterprise; protecting the people from teachers who, either through ignorance or intentional error, would lead God's chosen people into misconceptions of God and misunderstandings of what it is that God desires and demands of the faithful.

Therefore, this is an attack by Jesus, but we must not misunderstand what and who is being attacked. First, it is not the common Jewish person, for he/she trusts that the leaders are faithfully communicating God's will to them. If the common people are blind, it is not a purposeful blindness. Neither is it an attack on the "word of God." Rather it is an attack on the religious leader's interpretations and teaching of the word of God.

Does this story, then, label Jesus (or the author of the gospel) as anti-Semitic or even anti-Judaic? The obvious answer is no. What we have here is a confrontation between a relatively unknown Jewish religious teacher challenging established Jewish religious leaders over the value and virtue of long-held religious traditions. The suspicion each holds for each other escalates, and, in the end, in this story, Jesus warns the leaders and the people who are witnessing this confrontation of mishandling the word of God, the consequences of which the religious leaders cannot possibly accept.

Mt 12.38–45 (cf. Lk 11.24–26, 29–32): In Mt 12, the scribes and Pharisees address Jesus with the respected title "teacher" (Gr = Διδάσκαλε = rabbi). However, they are still uncertain as to who He is or where He is from. It is possible, then, that it is this uncertainty rather than some dark plot by the religious leaders which motivates them to ask for a "sign from You." What sign Jesus could have produced that would have convinced them of His origins is uncertain. However, the author(s) of the gospel of Matthew portrays Jesus as being irritated with this question, obviously seeing this as another attempt to trap or trick Jesus into saying something that they might use against him at some later date. The response of Jesus is couched in images and stories from the Hebrew Scriptures—the repentance of the pagan Ninevites in response to the preaching of Jonah and the pagan Queen of Sheba blessing Solomon's God following her conversation with Solomon.[68] However, not only will both the Ninevites and the Queen of Sheba "rise in the judgment with this [wicked (v.45)] generation to condemn it," but one "greater" than Jonah (a prophet) and Solomon (a king)—the "Son of Man"—"is here." This, of course, would have been entirely unacceptable to the religious leaders, who saw themselves as the spiritual (and physical) progeny of the heroes of Israel's past. For this unlearned man to imagine that a pagan nation and a pagan queen could sit in judgment of them, the chosen of God, was simply beyond comprehension. What we have here, then, is Jesus, in the hearing of the religious leaders, in unmistakable language, declaring his understanding of who He is. And it is entirely possible, that the scribes and Pharisees heard Jesus naming himself as the long-looked for Messiah. Further, it was inconceivable that the promised Messiah, who was to deliver God's chosen people from their evil oppressors, would name the Jewish people as a "wicked" generation deserving of condemnation.

Mt 13.36–43: In this passage, Jesus says to his disciples that He, "the Son of Man, will send out his angels" (τοὺς ἀγγέλους αὐτοῦ) to assist Him in a final judgment of those who "offend and those who practice lawlessness . . . at the end of this age." Therefore, Jesus is saying that He, the "Son of Man," has the authority to bring a judgment of fire, and that the angels, believed (at least by the Pharisees) to be supernatural, are answerable to Him.

A fragment from the commentary on this passage from Theodore of Mopsuestia, however, offers a rare "olive branch" to the Jewish people here.

> [Jesus] calls Greeks, Jews and Samaritans "three measures of meal," for then the leaven had been cast into these three it brought about one same nature and

fatness in all of them. For human beings, divided from one another, were brought into the same state by my teaching, in its working. The apostle also speaks in the same way, for "in Christ Jesus" there is neither "Greek" nor "Jew" and so on.[69]

Mt 16.13–17 (cf. Mk 8.31; Lk 9.20–22): When Jesus asks his disciples "who do men say that I, the Son of Man, am?" Peter's response is that while others think Jesus is one of the prophets, Peter believes Jesus to be "the Christ (ὁ χριστὸς; Heb = "messiah"), the Son of the living God."[70] For Peter, then, the "Son of Man" is the "Son of God." Therefore, if this story is not a later redaction,[71] perhaps the most interesting point of the story is that Jesus does not upbraid Peter for being blasphemous (cf. Mt 26.62–65) but in fact tells him that the Father of the "Son of the living God" revealed this to Peter. In other words, to come to an understanding that this "Son of Man" is the divine Son of God is a divine revelation. Epiphanius the Latin would later write that it was through faith that "the Gentiles rather than the Jews would come to acknowledge the Son of God."[72] He goes on to say that "the Jews did not believe that he was the Son of God but regarded him merely as the son of Joseph."[73] This, of course, was why Jesus was accused of blasphemy. He was the son of a carpenter and nothing more.

Taking every opportunity to defame and accuse the Jewish leaders of malice, Chrysostom points out that Jesus did not ask His disciples who the Scribes and Pharisees thought He was but the common people for "even if common opinion was far less true than might have been, at was as least relatively more free from malice than the opinions of the religious leaders, which was teeming with bad motives."[74]

On the question of Jesus being both the Son of Man and the Son of God, later Christians were not troubled by Jesus being both. Theodore of Heraclea wrote, "[It is] not as if he were divided into different species, one part God and one part man; rather one may address him as Son of Man with no doubt that this very same one is also the Son of God."[75]

Mt 16.21–28: Most of the main protagonists of Jesus and his ministry up to this point in Matthew's gospel, that is, the elders, chief priests, and scribes, are, not surprisingly, identified here as the ones responsible for the crucifixion of Jesus. However, the use of the word translated "must" (δεῖ; lit. "it is necessary") in v.21 implies that although the elders, chief priests, and scribes will be involved in his crucifixion, his death is a necessary element of a divinely predetermined purpose that cannot be fulfilled without the death of Jesus. For without his death, there can be no resurrection, and many early Christian soteriologies were predicated on the substitutionary death and resurrection of Jesus. Therefore, although the death of Jesus can be (and has been) read as the successful culmination of the plottings of the enemies of Jesus, this passage (and others) strongly suggest, rather, that the crucifixion was the intention of Jesus; His very *raison d'etre*, and those who were actually involved in the death of Jesus, were merely players in a much larger drama that had a divine origin. This argument is further strengthened by both Lk 17.24–25 and Jhn 3.14, where Jesus uses the same word. "δεῖ," to speak of His suffering and death. In the passage in Luke, Jesus tells His disciples that the "Son of Man . . . must" suffer many things, and be rejected, and in John 3.14, Jesus uses the imagery of the serpent lifted up by Moses in the wilderness to say that the "Son of Man . . . must" also be lifted up so that "whoever believes in Him should not perish but have eternal life." In Mt 20.28 (cf. Mk 10.45), Jesus says the "Son of Man" came to this earth "to give His life a ransom for many." It was always His and God's intention that He come to die for His people. Seen, therefore, from this perspective, the charge of deicide leveled against the Jewish people for centuries is unsupportable and must finally be abandoned, for it is not even supported by the Christians' own sacred scriptures.

This argument is further strengthened in Jhn 10.17–18, where Jesus declares in unequivocal language that He, and He alone, has power over both his own life and death. He says, "My Father loves Me, because I lay down my life. . . . No one takes it from Me, but I lay it down of Myself. I have the power to lay it down, and I have the power to take it again. This command I received from My Father." In other words, none of his enemies, either alone or together, can do anything to him that he alone allows. As the "good shepherd [who] gives His life for the sheep," (v.11) Jesus is enacting the *heils geschicte* that both He and God had intended. He is telling those listening to Him (including some Pharisees) that He is fulfilling the "command [which He] received from [His] Father" and that His death is blessed by God. Therefore, it is curious that the very event (the crucifixion) that many Christians believe delivers them from the guilt and power of sin, also elicits in them hostility and hatred against those who, from this perspective, are guiltless.

That this predetermined death of Jesus as the means of providing salvation for God's people was foreordained by God is seen in two other passages in the Gospel of Matthew, and many passages in the book of Acts, and in the epistles.[76]

There is fairly convincing evidence in these two passages in Matthew that Jesus, because of His self-understanding, was able to read many of the prophesies found in the Hebrew Scriptures as applicable to Him. In the parable of the landowner in Mt 21, God is the landowner; the sent servants who are beaten, stoned, and killed are former prophets, priests, kings, etc., who have been faithful to God; and the son, who is cast from the vineyard and killed, is Jesus. The son, then, in this parable, is the personification of the chief cornerstone of the quoted Ps 118.22–23, which the builders rejected. However, this rejection of the chief cornerstone is "the Lord's doing, And it is marvelous in our eyes." What Jesus is implying is that not only did God know that the sent Son would be rejected but that this scenario was designed by Him. Therefore, while there can be other interpretations of this parable, if the interpretation offered above is considered, it becomes extremely difficult, if not impossible, to charge the Jewish leaders with deicide. That Jesus was sent by God to provide atonement for sins is also supported by the Apostle Paul. In one of many passages that speak to this reality, Paul says that "*God set forth [Jesus]* to be a propitiation (ἱλαστήριον; lit "to turn away wrath") *by his blood*, through faith, to demonstrate His righteousness" (Rom 3.25; emphasis added). Therefore, it seems that early Christians believed that neither God nor Jesus was surprised by the turn of events that led to His crucifixion, for they believed that this was God's intention.[77]

In Jhn 10.11 Jesus says, "I am the good shepherd. The good shepherd gives His life for the sheep." In v.14 he repeats, "I am the good shepherd . . . and I lay down My life for the sheep." In Mt 26.31, on the eve of the trail and crucifixion of Jesus, He reprises this imagery using Zech 13.7: "I will strike the Shepherd, And the sheep of the flock will be scattered." The context of this passage, on the eve of the crucifixion, seems to suggest that the Shepherd being struck is Jesus. And since in Jhn 10.17-18, Jesus declares that no one can take His life, the person doing the striking of the Shepherd is God.

The contemporary context of the passage in Zech 13 is both judgment and redemption for Israel, and that judgment and redemption is preceded by the striking of the shepherd. It is possible that Jesus, already believing Himself to be the good shepherd who lays down His life for His flock, understands Himself to be reenacting this judgment/redemption scenario from Zech 13. In this reenactment He is the shepherd, and the one doing the striking is God, and if the sheherd is struck the sheep will scatter, but the shepherd must be struck. In fact, it may be possible to suggest that judgment and redemption cannot come unless the shepherd is struck. This is a possible interpretation, and it (or ones closely similar) is one which has had a sizable hearing throughout the twenty centuries of Christianity. What needs to be said here, then, is that those who accept this interpretation are guilty of no less than cognitive dissonance if they also continue to charge the Jewish people with deicide. They cannot have it both ways. The Jews and the Romans are either instruments of their own evil and demonic forces, or they are instruments in the hands of God, bringing to fulfillment God's own plan for the redemption of humanity.

The clearest evidence, which points to the crucifixion as a divinely predetermined event, is found in Acts 2.23, where Peter, at Pentecost, in Jerusalem, not speaking in metaphors, but in history, rehearsing the events leading up to the crucifixion of Jesus, and the consequences of His death, says that Jesus was delivered up "by the determined counsel and foreknowledge of God." This rather straightforward declaration of Peter's hardly needs any analysis, but coupled with the textual evidence already discussed, the Jewish leaders are only guilty of allowing themselves to be used by God in a predetermined plan to bring deliverance to God's people (including the Jewish people).

Therefore, while there is unmistakable evidence that the Jewish leaders' attitude toward Jesus went from mild annoyance to outright hatred—a hatred that led to plots against his life—there is also unmistakable evidence that it was the Roman officials under the direction of Pontius Pilate who put Jesus to death on the cross. But the evidence from the Gospels and the book of Acts is also unmistakable; *viz.* that Jesus, acting in concert with God, was sent to the earth to die, and that His death was meant to be propitious. The divine judgment that was to fall on humanity fell substitutionarily on Jesus.

Mt 17.1–13, 22–23 (cf. Mk 9.2–9; Lk 9.28–36[78]): The passage here in the synoptics adds to the picture of the "Son of Man" as a (or the) suffering servant, who will not only suffer but also be treated with contempt. The passage here is proceeded by what has commonly been called the "transfiguration"—a vision of a beatific Jesus with Moses and Elijah, witnessed by Peter, James, and John, in which the voice of God says, "This is my beloved Son. Hear Him!" (Gr = ἀκούετε αὐψοῦ; lit.—"listen to him!"). As they come down from the mountain, Jesus commands the disciples to tell no one of the experience until the "Son of Man had risen from the dead." It is because the disciples later ask Jesus, "Why do the scribes say that Elijah must come first?" that we can conclude that even though they did not fully understand what "rising from the dead meant," they are beginning to accept that the "Son of Man" is the coming Messiah.[79]

Jesus compares His future treatment with that of Elijah, and He recalls that "they (the political and spiritual leaders of the Jewish people in the 8th c. B.C.E.) did to him whatever they wished." The stories tell us that Elijah was taken into heaven without seeing death, but before this happened he was constantly hounded and had a price on his head. Therefore, this is an attempt either by Jesus or the writer of the gospel or a later redactor to say that as the messengers from God were treated in the past, so will be the "Son of Man."

This same language of murder and resurrection is repeated later in ch.17 when Jesus tells His disciples, "The Son of Man is about to be betrayed into the hands of men, and they will kill Him, and the third day He will be raised up." However, while in v.12 He implies that it will be the Jewish people who will cause the "Son of Man . . . to suffer at their hands," in v.22, he is betrayed into the hands of the more generic "men." This, therefore, could be read to imply that more than just a group of first century enemies are going to be responsible for His death.

Jhn 8.12–59: If in the Gospel of John the chapters leading up to ch.8 can be seen as sparring between Jesus and the religious leaders, in ch.8, the gloves come off, and both Jesus and the religious leaders go at each other. By the time we arrive at John 8, both Jesus and the religious leaders have reached an unspoken understanding that they can neither allow themselves, nor the rest of the people of Israel, to perceive them as two mutually accepted messengers of God's will and truth. The divine acceptance and approbation of one automatically earns Gods condemnation of the other. The validity of their competing claims rests on who has the strongest claim to a righteous spiritual heritage. Jesus continues to claim that God is His father (vv.16, 18, 19, 23, 26, 28, 29, 38, 40, 42, 49, 54, 55), while the religious leaders continue to state that they are the true heirs of Abraham, the father of the chosen people of God (vv.33, 39, 53). However, imbedded in these self-justifying claims are condemnations of the other. In this chapter, Jesus either directly accuses or implies that the religious leaders "walk in darkness" (v.12), are unable to recognize a divine messenger from God (v.14), "judge according to the flesh" (v.15; over against the spirit?), do not know the Father (v.19, 55), will die in their sins (v.21, 24), are from beneath (as opposed to above?) and of this world (as opposed to heaven?; v.23), are judged by Jesus (v.26), are slaves who will not inherit eternal life (vv.34,35), do not do the works of Abraham (vv.39, 40), seek to kill God's messengers (v.40), have the desires of the devil, a murderer and a liar, as their father (v.44), do not believe the truth (v.45), do not hear God's words (v.47), are not of God (v.47), and are liars (v.55). The Jewish leaders in turn accuse Jesus of being a false witness (v.13), a child of the sin of fornication (v.41), a Samaritan (v.48), being possessed by a demon (vv.48, 52), and incredibly self-important (v.53).

In the midst of this escalating war of words Jesus says in v.28, "When you lift up the Son of Man, then you will know that I am *He*, and that I do nothing of Myself." Because the word "*He*" is supplied, a more literal reading is, "When you lift up the Son of Man, then you will know that I am" (ἐγώ εἰμι). And while it can be argued that the word "He" is implied, in v.58, the entire argument with the Jewish leaders about who Jesus is concludes by Jesus declaring, " Most assuredly, I say to you, before Abraham was, I AM (ἐγώ εἰμι). Jesus is identifying himself as the "I AM" of the Hebrew Scriptures. Therefore, not only is the "Son of Man" the "Son of God;" He is God, which is of course why, in v.59, "they took up stones to throw at Him." This Jesus was, in the eyes of the Jewish leaders, guilty of the most obscene blasphemy. When they asked Him in v.53, "Whom do You make yourself out to be?" He answered that He was God. It seems, then, that there was little chance of some sort of reconciliation, or even rapprochement, between Jesus and the religious leaders following this confrontation.

Jhn 9.14–41: The next appearance of the term "Son of Man" is found in the very next chapter of John. It is not too difficult to conclude that the encounter of Jesus with the blind man immediately follows the events of ch.8, for when the Pharisees learn that it was Jesus who healed the man (on the Sabbath), they try to convince the healed man that Jesus is, in fact a sinner, and that he (the healed blind man) must give glory to God. When the man insists that it was Jesus who healed him, they accuse him of being "completely born in sins" and "cast him out" (of the Temple? synagogue?). Jesus, apparently, was not finished with the Pharisees for "some of the Pharisees [who] were with [Jesus]" (v.40) heard Jesus ask the man, "Do you believe in the Son of Man?" And the chapter concludes with Jesus stating that the "seeing" Pharisees are both blind and in their sins (v.41).

Lk 17.20–30: In Lk 17.20, Jesus is asked "by the Pharisees when the kingdom of God would come." Implicit in this question is the belief that the kingdom of God was not a present reality but a divinely established kingdom in the future. It seems unlikely that the Pharisees would ask Jesus this question unless it was just to see whether His response would be different from theirs. The other possibility is that the author of the gospel of Luke inserted this question here to give him (the author) the opportunity to voice his own beliefs about the kingdom of God.

The responses of Jesus are enigmatic, for in vv.20, 21, he says that the kingdom of God will "not come with observation," for indeed, the kingdom of God is within you (Gr = ἐντός; lit = "in the midst"). In other words, the kingdom of

God is not something to be looked for in the future but is a present reality. However, in the next few verses, the language about the "kingdom of God" changes into the "days of the Son of Man" (v.22) and the "day when the Son of Man is revealed." The implication here is that the kingdom of God begins "when the Son of Man is revealed." Further, as God destroyed the earth with water in the days of Noah, and Sodom and Gomorrah with fire and brimstone in the days of Lot, so the day of the "Son of Man" will be accompanied by a worldwide fiery conflagration. Therefore, if in first century Jewish teaching, some believed that God was the final judge of all things, and a restorer of the kingdom of God, Jesus is claiming that divine privilege, and this would, once again, make Him guilty of blasphemy. Further, Jesus says in this passage that escape from this final conflagration is not dependent upon a correct interpretation of the Torah or even a moral life. Escape, in fact, is the willingness to believe a paradox" "Whoever seeks to save his life will lose it, and whoever loses his life will preserve it" (v.33).

Lk 18.1–8: Lk 18 continues the teachings from Jesus that began in ch.17.20. Of the two parables found in ch.18, the first ends with Jesus asking, "Nevertheless, when the Son of Man comes, will He really (Gr = ἄρα; lit = then)[80] find faith on the earth?" It can be inferred from this question that there will be a time in the future when the "Son of Man" will come again; but this time as a judge, and as a judge He will be looking for faith but not really expecting to find any. The point being made, then, to the Pharisees (7.20), those who "trusted in them-selves that they were righteous" (8.9), His disciples (8.15), and a ruler (8.18), is that when the "kingdom of God . . . [does] come" (7.20), one of the things that the "Son of Man," as judge, will be looking for, but questions whether it will be found, is faith. Therefore, whatever loosing one's life of 7.33 meant, it also means having faith.

Two things need to be noted here. The disciples of Jesus heard this discourse as well as the Pharisees. Therefore, when Jesus questions whether He will find faith when He returns as judge, He is directing this not just to the religious leaders but to His own disciples as well.

Secondly, it cannot be concluded that faith was not an important element of Jewish religiosity and spirituality. For Christians to say that if you do not have faith in Jesus Christ, you do not have faith is to say to millions of non-Christians, including ancient and modern Jews, that their religion has no salvific value. Christians do not have the right to say that, and not only is it historically wrong, it is theologically reductionistic.

Mt 19.27–30 (cf. Mk 10.28–30; Lk 18.28–30): In this passage, Jesus says that He, as the "Son of Man," will "in the regeneration" (Gr = ἐν τῇ παλιγγενεσίᾳ; NRSV = "at the renewal of all things") be revealed as a glorious judge, sitting on "the throne of His glory." According to Thayer this word παλιγγενεσία "commonly . . . denotes *the restoration of a thing to its pristine state, its renovation,* as the renewal or restoration of life after death" (emphasis added). Further, it was the state of the world "which the Jews looked for in connection with the advent of the Messiah, and which the primitive Christians expected in connection with the visible return of Jesus from heaven."[81]

The use of the word "throne" speaks of authority or even royalty. Therefore, Jesus is announcing to his disciples that there is coming a restoration of all things, and at that time, He and His followers will sit in thrones, in judgment on the twelve tribes of Israel. However, many in Israel believed that the only one who could bring righteous judgment on Israel and the world was the Messiah of God. Jesus is saying that He is the one who will bring that judgment. The apostles, along with all of the Jewish people living in Palestine in the first century, knew that, although some high ranking Jewish officials had been given nominal political rights by the Romans to judge the Jewish people (mostly in matters of religion), that the only people who could bring judgment on the Jewish people were the Roman's themselves. Jesus is saying that "yes, judgment is coming, but it will not be the Romans who will be judging God's chosen people. It will, in fact be the Messiah, and those who are faithful to the Messiah, and leave all to follow Him will be rewarded in that judgment."

One ancient Christian, suspecting Jewish leaders at the time of judgment might try to escape that judgment writes the following:

> On the day of judgment the Jews will reply, "Lord, we did not know that you were the Son of God incarnate. For what man could see the treasure hidden in the earth or the sun hidden in a cloud? Who suspected that the morning star was born upon earth? Who thought that the woman who shut us out from paradise and prevented us all from entering it should herself become the first door of paradise? Or that the light should go forth through her who had caused the darkness to enter? And so it was not obstinacy of heart that drove us to injure you, but we were deceived by consideration of the flesh."
>
> You will reply to them, "We too were men just like you, having a similar soul and the same carnal nature, and we lived in one and the same world. We were threatened by the same factions of worldly spirits, helped by the same safeguards of God. Further, you had this advantage over us: we were simple unpolished men and sinners, and obscure in the crowd, while you were priests and scribes and leaders of the people. We, simple, rustic sinners, could recognize him. Even before witnessing his miracles, we understood him. But you, even after witnessing all his powers, could not understand him? How could it be that almost the whole race was ignorant of him whom Twelve knew? You did not believe him. You did not know that he was the Son of God. What caused you to kill him when you did not find any fault in him? In us the goodwill of our rustic ignorance was like a lantern. But in you, the malice of your knowledge enveloped you like darkness.[82]

The argument of this author is that while the Jewish leaders may want to plead ignorance, they should have known better, and it was those who were truly ignorant who were able to see through their ignorance and saw Jesus as the true Son of God. The ignorance of the Jewish leaders made them blind, while the ignorance of the Gentiles allowed them to see. This argument, then, is one more example of early Christian authors seeing nothing but impure and unrighteous motives behind the actions of the Jewish religious leaders.

Mt 20:17-19 (cf. Mk 10.32-34; Lk 18.31-34): As Jesus drew closer to his final confrontation with the Jewish and Roman authorities, his messages to his disciples about his impending death became more frequent. In what proved to be his final trip to Jerusalem, Jesus tells his disciples that they are on their way to Jerusalem, and there the "Son of Man" will be betrayed to the religious leaders who will condemn Him to death and deliver Him to the Gentiles who will crucify Him.

The disciples, by this time, had little doubt who Jesus was speaking of when he spoke of the "Son of Man." Although this portrayal of the "Son of Man" is completely contrary to the portrayal of the "Son of Man" in the previous chapter of Matthew, where He is seen as a coming judge, or more properly, "The Coming Judge," with the heavenly angels, to bring judgment on the wicked and unbelievers. How were the disciples to hear this? This is a portrayal of the Messiah that they would have never heard before their three-year odyssey with Jesus. However, if there were only one God, and that God was Jehovah, and Jesus was the Son of God, then this betrayal and death of the Son of God must have cosmic consequences. In v.28, He says that His death will not be just the death of another man, but that His death is given as a "ransom for many" (Gr = λύτρον ἀντὶ πολλῶν). A literal reading of the Greek ("a ransom instead of many") allows for the classical Christian understanding of the death of Jesus as substitutionary. Therefore, if that is the meaning of His words, then He is saying that His death does, indeed, have cosmic consequences.

How the disciples understood these words of Jesus is not recorded, but it must have been one of the stories about Jesus that was told and retold before the Gospels were written. Therefore, one of the questions that can be asked about this passage is this: was this story a later interpolation by the writers of the Gospels in an attempt to further blame and shame the Jews for the death of their Lord? If that is the case, then the blaming of the Jews for the crucifixion of Jesus, at least in these passages, comes from later Christian authors and not from Jesus. If, however, this is a faithful recording of the conversation between Jesus and his disciples, then Jesus is letting his disciples know that, although they believe Him to be the promised coming Messiah, He will still allow Himself to be betrayed and killed. Yet, again,, as in previous chapters, Jesus says that His death is not permanent, and, in this particular passage, He will raise from the dead three days following His crucifixion. It can be argued, then, that Jesus is attempting, at least with His disciples, to redefine who the Messiah was and what His experience was to be.

Mt 20.25-28: This is a truly remarkable passage for Jesus says here that the "Son of Man," whom He has previously told His disciples will come with the angels of God to bring glory to Himself and God, and to bring judgment, compares Himself to a slave (δοῦλος) whose death will be a ransom (λύτρον; lit = the price paid for redeeming slaves)[83] for many. This could have been quite difficult for the disciples to understand, for they had already declared Him to be the

"Son of God," the "King of Israel," and the "Messiah." Jesus had told them that His resurrection would usher in the time of glory and restoration; that He would, with them, be the righteous judges of God on the wicked. Examples of godly men offering their lives as a ransom for the sins of the people were not unheard of in Israel (Moses being one example), but was this to be one of the signs of the Messiah?

Jhn 12.23–36: Jhn 3.14 is not the only passage in the gospel of John where Jesus says that the "Son of Man must be lifted up." He also uses the phrase twice in ch.12 (vv.32, 34). However, while the audience in ch.3 was Nicodemus only, the audience in Jhn 12 includes gentiles, the disciples, and "people who stood by." There is no mention of religious leaders being present here.

It seems that the people understood that as the "Son of Man," Jesus was claiming to be the Messiah and that "being lifted up" meant that He was talking about being crucified, for they ask, "We have heard from the law that the Christ remains forever (Gr = μένει εἰς τὸν αἰνα; lit = "into the age"); and how can You say, 'The Son of Man must be lifted up?'" It can be extrapolated, then, that for some of the Jewish people in the first century, one of the characteristics of the Messiah was that he possessed eternal life in a way that others did not. Therefore, a person claiming to be the Messiah cannot be lifted up to be crucified. Yet, in both this passage and in Jhn 3, Jesus does not say that He "will" be lifted up, but He "must" (Gr = δεῖ; lit = "it is necessary") be lifted up. It seems as though for Jesus there is no choice. To accomplish what He was sent by God to do, He "must" be lifted up. Further, Jesus believes His crucifixion to be a (the?) time of judgment, for "now (νῦν) is the judgment of this world; now (νῦν) the ruler of this world will be cast out." Jesus also believes that through His crucifixion both the "Son of Man" (v.23) and the Father (v.28) will be glorified. This, of course, strengthens the argument that the death of Jesus was a divinely planned event that has exceedingly important and cosmic conesquences. Therefore, again, to blame the Jewish people for the death of Jesus is an excuse to exercise a religious and/or racial bigotry against a people who have suffered at the hands of Christians for over 2,000 years. It is purposeful blindness to what Christians claim to be their Holy Scriptures to ignore the words of their Lord with regards to His death. He "must be lifted up." The Apostle Paul understood this. He repeatedly speaks of the necessity of Jesus Christ dieing for our sins. In Rom 8.32, 34 he wrote, "He who did not spare His own Son, but delivered Him up for us all, how shall He not with Him also freely give us all things? . . . It is Christ who died, and furthermore is also risen, who is even at the right hand of God, who also makes intercession for us." He repeats this theme throughout Romans, 1 and 2 Corinthians, and in 1 Thessalonians. Further, the author of the Epistle to the Hebrews wrote, "So Christ was offered once to bear the sins of many" (9.28).

Jhn 13.31–35: After Judas leaves Jesus and the disciples in the "upper room," Jesus says to the rest of the disciples, "Now the Son of Man is glorified, and God is glorified in Him." While the disciples may not have understood what Jesus was saying, the traditional Christian understanding of these words of Jesus is that He is, once again, in different language, telling the disciples of His impending death, and that it is in His death, both He and the Father will be glorified. And although the specific meaning of the words of Jesus can be debated, the subtext is that His own glorification will also bring glorification to God, thus strengthening His union with God. In the next few hours, Jesus will be vilified by many and abandoned by His closest friends, but "now," at the Passover Feast, both He, as the "Son of Man," and God will be glorified.

Mt 26.57–68 (cf. Mk 14.53–65; Lk 22.66–71): This story is the final use of the term "Son of Man" by Jesus. Word had obviously reached the high priest that this Jesus was making claims about Himself that were blasphemous. Others had made similar claims, but the claims of Jesus were accompanied with scathing denunciations and even divine condemnations of both these leaders and the present generation. Jesus had, by this time, made it abundantly clear that He had no desire to join the Jewish leaders in leading the Jewish people or to support them in their own continued work. His self-understanding was now so complete that when the high priest demanded, "I adjure you by the living God that You tell us if You are the Christ (Messiah), the Son of God," Jesus confirmed his suspicions by declaring, "It is as you said" (σὺ εἶπας; v.63b–64a). And because He is the Christ, the Son of God, they will hereafter "see the Son of Man sitting at the right hand of power, and coming in the clouds of heaven" (v.64b). The high priest declares the words of Jesus to be blasphemous and Jesus to be a blasphemer, and when he asks the onlookers what should be done, they reply, "He is deserving of death" (v.66b). This was, of course, according to the Torah, the proscribed penalty for blasphemy.[84]

The words put into the mouths of "all the people" that the blood of Jesus "be on us and on our children" are words that Christians have used as justifycation for their persecution of the Jewish people for generation after generation. Christians have exacted the blood of countless Jews for what the Christians have believed to be the Jewish peoples own self-proscribed penalty: "His blood be on us and on our children." And because this self-damning curse does not have a terminus, there can never be a time when the "children" of the first century Jews responsible for the crucifixion of Jesus are free from it. Therefore, whether or not these words were actually voiced, Christians have believed that they were voiced, and these words have haunted Jewish/Christian relations for the past 2000 years.[85]

Matthew 26 and 27 is devoted to establishing the intent of the "the chief priests, the scribes, and the elders" (v.26.3), "the chief Priests" (v.26.14), "the chief priests and elders of the people" (v.26.47), "the chief priests, the elders, and all the council" (v.26.59), "the high priest" (v.26.65), the "chief priests and elders" (27.1), the "chief priests and elders" (27.20), and the "chief priests . . . with [the] scribes and elders" (27.41) to have Jesus killed. Matthew's portrayal of the Jewish leaders in ch.26 and 27 is that they, because of their hatred of Jesus, have become more than just instruments of God to fulfill God's will. Through money, trickery, and false testimony, they are intent on the death of Jesus. The readers of Mt 26 and 27 are presented with a picture of a group of people who have been, heretofore, frustrated in fulfilling their own designs in silencing Jesus, and are now focused on one goal: putting Jesus to death.

The aim of the author(s) of the Gospel of Matthew in ch.26 and 27 is to make sure that the readers know and understand that all of the enemies of Jesus, that is, Judas (Mt 26.14–15, 47 (cf. Mk 14.10–11; Lk 22.3–6), the Roman officials (Mt 27.20, 22, 24b–25; cf. Mk 15.11–12; Lk 23.13–24 Jhn 19.6–16), and the religious leaders (Mt 26.1, 2–4; cf. Mk 14.1; Lk 22.1–2); Mt 26.59-60a (cf. Mk 14.56); Mt 26.65-68 (cf. Mk 14.63–65; Lk 22.63, 71); Mt 27.1 (cf. Mk 15.1); and Mt 27.39, 41 (cf. Mk 15.29–31; Lk 23.34–35), share culpability in the crucifixion. Judas is portrayed as a pathetic opportunist who sells his loyalty to the religious leaders, and the Roman officials are seen as almost disinterested instruments in the hands of the religious leaders. However, while later Christians dismiss Judas and turn their backs on the Romans, the Jewish people, and especially the Jewish leaders, become the objects of an especial hatred. The theories as to why Christians turned their backs to the Romans but turned on the Jews are fairly well known, but they bear repeating here.

The argument is that the Romans can almost be excused for their part in the death of Jesus because they did not know any better. They were poor benighted pagans, whose minds were darkened by centuries of believing fables. However, the Jewish people had been called by God to be His chosen people. Many of the Christians believed that the Tanakh was a continual indictment against the people whom God strove with for hundreds of years. The Tanakh, to these Christians, proved that the Jewish people were truly a "stiff-necked" people, who were bent on self-destruction by continually rejecting God and His messengers. Origen writes that the Jewish leaders were motivated by Satan and worked in league with him bringing about the death of Jesus. He writes that the High Priest "committed a sin in plotting against Jesus. Therefore, he was of the devil, and being of the devil, as it were, he imitated his very father."[86] Two centuries later, this accusation continues to be heard, this time from Jerome, who writes, "Blind anger and impatience, bereft of grounds for a false accusation, dislodged the high priest from his seat, and he displayed the rabid state of his mind with a vehement bodily gesture."[87] Leo the Great[88], Cyril of Alexandria[89], and Chrysostom[90], among others, also contributed to a growing corpus of Christian literature that accused the Jewish leaders of the worst of sins in the crucifixion of Jesus.

However, the Jewish religious leaders, in the first century C.E., read their sacred scripture as evidence that the ancient covenant with God was still intact and that they were still God's special people. God's divine truth; the only truth given to humanity, was entrusted to them and no one else. No one else had either the right or ability to understand the true God and their God's dealings with humanity, and this was most especially true of those whom they believed were unwisely following a false messiah.

In conclusion, the disciples heard Jesus referring to Himself as the "Son of Man" from the very beginning to the very end of their three years together. The disciples could hardly mistake His use of this self-identifying term as a way of revealing to them His identity as the Messiah. For in the texts reviewed, Jesus lets His disciples know that He has a relationship with the heavenly angels, the past heroes of Israel, and even God, that other faithful Jews do not have, and while all male Jews in the first century could speak of themselves as "sons of God," Jesus identifies himself as "the" "Son of God."

While many Jews in first century Palestine wished for and prayed for judgment to fall on their Roman oppressors, Jesus says that He, in the future, will bring a final judgment on all of creation. Further, while dying defending the promised land would be considered a noble death for all first century Jewish people, and bring honor to that hero, the death of the "Son of Man" for all of humanity has far greater cosmic consequences. Therefore, while Jesus reinforces some of the traditional understandings of the Messiah, as judge and deliverer, there emerges a picture of the Messiah as a suffering servant, who will allow Himself to be judged by those over whom He has power. Not only is there a coming glory, accompanied with divine judgment, but there is a time of humiliation and death. Yet it is through this death that the "Son of Man" actually achieves the glory that is His due.

Conclusion

These, then, are the texts in which Jesus reveals to His disciples and others His self-understanding of who He was, especially in the context of His self-naming term the "Son of Man." They can be grouped into the following categories:

A) His unique relationship with heaven:

1) Jhn 1.47–51: Jesus is some sort of a conduit from both heaven to earth and earth to heaven for the angels of God.

2) Jhn 3.11–21: Jesus was sent by God and came down from heaven.

3) Mt 12.22–37: Jesus claims that His miracles are performed through the power of the Holy Spirit, and while speaking against Him will be forgiven, speaking against the Holy Spirit will not. It is difficult, however, to imagine that the Jewish leaders would not hear, in this statement of Jesus, the connection between Him and the Holy Spirit.[91]

4) Mt 13.36–43: With the angels of God Jesus will bring a fiery judgment on those that offend and practice lawlessness. The claim of Jesus, here, was not uncommon. The Jewish leaders were aware that God had used individuals (judges, prophets, kings) and peoples (Babylonians, Assyrians) to bring judgment both for and against Israel in the past. Therefore, Jesus may have been viewed at this time as another zealot who mistakenly thought He was the instrument of God to cleanse Israel of her sins. However, judgment was ultimately in the hands of God, and Jesus is saying that God had chosen Him to be God's agent in a coming, final judgment.

5) Mt 16.27–28: Jesus, in the future, accompanied by the angels of God, "in the glory of the Father," will come to bring judgment.

B) His unique relationship with God: Jesus implies that he has a relationship with the God of Israel that far exceeds that of the religious leaders and in fact exceeds even that of the Prophets of the Hebrew Scriptures. For the faithful believers in Israel, an acceptance of this proposition is, by implication, a negation of what the Jewish people believe to be an accurate portrayal of history. They are not being asked to reject what is sacred but to accept a radical reinterpretation of their sacred scriptures and traditions.

1) Mt 12.38–45 (cf. Lk 11.24–26, 29–32): Present day (first century) Israel will, in the Day of Judgment, be judged and condemned by the heathen Ninevites of Jonah's day, for while the Ninevites repented at Jonah's preaching, one greater than Jonah, a prophet of God (see II Ki 14.25), is rejected by them. Therefore, Jesus is claiming that He is greater than a prophet (or all prophets?) of God.

2) Mt 16.13–17 (cf. Mk 8.31; Lk 9.20–2): When Peter declares his belief that Jesus is the Christ (Messiah), the Son of the living God, Jesus blesses Peter, and tells him that God revealed that truth to him.

3) Jhn 13.31–35: On the night of His trial, Jesus says that He is glorified by God, and He is glorified in God, and this will be done "immediately" (Gr = ἐυθὺς; lit = "forthwith").

C) He is the judge of both Israel and the world: Judgment against the wicked oppressors of Israel was a theme that occupied many in Israel. However, judgment, from God, against Israel for disobedience of His requirements was also a popular literary subject. Jesus says in these passages that in the coming judgment, which apparently was already a given, He is the judge of all.

1) Mt 16.27–28: When the "Son of Man" comes "in His kingdom" in the "glory of His Father with His angels," He will reward each according to their works.

2) Jhn 9.14–41: Not only will Jesus come as Judge at the End of Days but "for judgment I have come into this world." A careful reading of the passage makes it clear that the judgment is on sin.

3) Mt 19.27–30 (cf. Mk 10.28–30; Lk 18.28–30): When God returns the world to its original state of perfection through the "regeneration" (Gr = παλιγγενεσίᾳ), Jesus and his followers will be sitting on thrones to judge, not just the world, but particularly the twelve tribes of Israel.

4) Mt 26.57–68 (cf. Mk 14.53–65; Lk 22.66–71): At some point in the future, Jesus will return as a judge, coming on the clouds of heaven, sitting at the right hand of power (God?).

5) Lk 17.20–30: The end of all things and the ushering in of the kingdom of God coincides at the future coming of the "Son of Man" with judgment.

6) Lk 18.1–8: The implication from Jesus' question, "Will He really find faith on the earth," is that He will come to make a judgment with regard to that question.

D) He is the Savior of both Israel and the world:

1) Jhn 3.11–21: Four times in four verses, Jesus states that salvation is possible through belief in Him or through Him, and the imagery of being lifted up strongly suggests that this salvation will be made available through His crucifixion.

2) Mt 9.2–8: If in first century Palestinian Judaism, salvation consisted of forgiveness of sin, which could only come from God, then when Jesus tells the paralytic that his sins are forgiven Jesus is, in essence, declaring Himself to be the Savior.

3) Jhn 5.19–47: Jesus' statements that "the Son gives life to whom He will," belief in Him brings "everlasting life," and the dead hearing His voice and coming to life, are statements that many first century Palestinian Jews would believe come from God acting as Savior.

4) Mt 13.36–43: Jesus is the Sower of good seeds who are the "sons of the kingdom" and who fall onto the world; the harvest is at the "end of the age" and the good seed will escape the judgment of those who will be "cast into the furnace of fire."

5) Jhn 6.26–71: Jesus says that He is "the bread of God" that gives life to the dead in the Day of Judgment and that life is everlasting. Those who eat His flesh and drink His blood, which He "gives for the life of the world," have eternal life. They will "live because of Me."

6) Jhn 8.12–59: Among the words of Jesus in this passage are the following:

> v.24: "If you do not believe that I am *He* ("He" is supplied; Gr = ἐγώ εἰμι; lit = "I am"), you will die in your sins."
> v.51: "If anyone keeps My word he shall never see death."

7) Mt 19.27–30: Jesus clearly associates the time of regeneration with a time of salvation, and He says to His disciples, "You who have followed Me . . . [will] inherit everlasting life."

8) Mt 20.25–28: When Jesus says that He came to "give His life a ransom for many," He is saying that He believes that His death will be the payment due to God to redeem those who might otherwise face God's wrath in the judgment.[92]

9) Jhn 12.23–36: Thayer reasons that while ὑψοω means "to lift on high, to exalt," with ἐκ τῆς γῆς added, the phrase becomes "to remove (lit = *out of*) the earth by crucifixion."[93] Therefore, when Jesus says in v.31 that His crucifixion will draw all people to Himself; given what He already has said about His purpose for coming to the earth, He is talking about His crucifixion providing salvation for all humanity.

E) He is the God of both Israel and the world:

1) Mt 9.2–6 (cf. Mk 2.1–7; Lk 5.17–21): Jesus is accused of blasphemy when He assumes a divine prerogative by forgiving the sins of a paralytic, a right reserved only for God.

2) Jhn 5.19–47: Only God can give life, and in this passage, Jesus claims that power for Himself in v.21; "The Son gives life to whom He will."

3) John 6.26–71: Whatever Jesus means by announcing Himself as the "bread of life," He has the blessings of God, and indeed the prerogatives of God. He, here and in Jhn 5, in unmistakable language, declares that He has mastery over life and death.

4) Jhn 8.12–59: In the middle of this long, rather heated exchange between Jesus and the religious leaders, Jesus declares that He is God and that the religious leaders are of Satan. This statement leaves them no options but to condemn Him as a blasphemer and guilty of death.

5) Mt 20.25–28 (cf. Mk 10.45): The Son of Man is responsible for the salvation of His people, but in this passage, He can only accomplish that through His death.

6) Lk 17.20–30; 18.1–8: The language in these passages strongly suggests that Jesus, as the "Son of Man," is responsible for bringing the world to an end, and the beginning of the kingdom of God.

F) He is self-existent: In these passages, Jesus reveals that, even though He has a very special relationship with heaven and heavenly beings, is the promised Messiah, and is, in fact, God—the God who will come again to judge both Israel and the world—He will be put to death. However, death will only contain Him for three days. Jesus is not saying He is deathless, just that He will not remain dead.

1) Mt 17.1–13 (cf. Mk 9.2–9; Lk 9.28–36): Jesus, like Elijah and John the Baptist, will suffer at the hands of men, be killed by them, but will rise from the dead.

2) Mt 20:17–19 (cf. Mk 10.32–34; Lk 18.31–34): The combined enemies of Jesus, including the gentiles and Jews, will condemn Jesus, put Him to death, but He will rise to life on the third day.

Therefore, the question that presents itself is, how did the disciples, religious leaders and common people understand what Jesus was saying about Himself when He used the term "Son of Man?" When he talked about His unique relationship with heaven, He used language that implied that He was the only person who had that relationship. It can be suggested that most in Israel would have believed that if anyone had a special relationship with heaven, it would have been the priests and rabbis. However, not only does Jesus say that He has a special relationship with heaven but that the religious leaders, because of their unbelief, have separated themselves from God and have sacrificed their rights and obligations to lead the people of God. He says that because of their unbelief, they have revealed their true character and their true spiritual heritage, and it is not heavenly. One cannot expect the religious leaders, nor some of the common people, simply to accept these words of Jesus. The New Testament is often read in a way that suggests that all of the common people were supporters of Jesus, and while it is probably true that many did accept Him, to suggest that the religious leaders had no supporters, especially in their conflicts with Jesus, is naïve. So when Jesus makes some of these accusations, there would have been many people who would seen Him as being either delusional or self-important.

This is also true when Jesus talks about His unique relationship with God—a relationship that may even surpass that of some of the spiritual heroes of Israel.

It is His claims of judgeship at the end of the age, or at the coming of the kingdom, or at the regeneration, with the angels and blessings of God, that most clearly identifies Him with some of the most common ideas about the Messiah. However, while these claims may have annoyed the religious leaders, and caused them to challenge His claims, Jesus was not the first person to claim to either be the Messiah or be hailed as the Messiah. There were others previous, and there may have been others after His time. Whether the others who claimed to be the promised Messiah also referred to themselves as the "Son of Man" is not known, but Jesus' use of that term, along with other claims would lead many to hear Him claiming to be the Messiah.

However, while these other claims of who the "Son of Man" was might have been cause for concern, it was Jesus' claims that He was both the Savior of both Israel and the world, and further that He was the very God of both Israel and the world that caused the most damage between Him and the religious leaders. The statements of Jesus that He, and only He, was the Savior of Israel, and the entire world; that He was the person who could give eternal life; that He was the God of the Tanakh was unthinkable to many in Israel, and was met with charges of blasphemy. This was not about theology but about divinity. One cannot be surprised that the overwhelming majority of religious leaders rejected the claims of Jesus. Later Christian claims that the rejection was because of a variety of spiritual diseases simply cannot be taken at face value. Therefore, these claims, along with the claim that Jesus was self-existent, led them all to the events now known as the crucifixion of Jesus on Golgotha.

As the writers of the gospels that came to be canonical wrote about the life of Jesus, they did so from a historical vantage point but a vantage point that was also historically contextualized. By the time the writers of these gospels wrote the biography of Jesus, the hostility that was demonstrated at the end of the life of Jesus had not gone away, nor was it forgotten. In fact, there is clear evidence that it increased, so that in the gospels, the reaction of the religious leaders to the claims of Jesus are seen in the most unflattering light possible. Motives are questioned; spiritual value is negated, and spiritual legacy is ignored.

Those who believe that the canonical gospels were written by Matthew, Mark, Luke, and John must then ask the question, are these men guilty of anti-Judaism and anti-Semitism? Are they guilty of unleashing centuries of hatred that is undiminished to this day? In what may sound like an effort to safeguard my own faith, I must answer "no" for the following reasons.

First, the Apostles were writing from their perspective. It is clear that they were angry and even suspicious about the Jewish leaders and their motives. They simply could not imagine how any people who were exposed to Jesus for all those years could deny His divinity. It was incomprehensible to them that His miracles and teachings did not awaken in the hearts of the historical people of God a response that was not dissimilar to theirs. The gospel writers were so convinced of the truth of their own understandings that any other understanding must come from purposeful recalcitrance, and once that belief about the Jewish leaders and people is established, other nefarious motives are imagined and lay behind actions that in another light may seem far less innocuous. Therefore, the apostles were either careful or uncareful with their language and interpretation of events. I am not saying that what they reported was untrue, but they wrote about them, at times, in ways that portrayed the religious leaders of first century Israel as villains.

However, having said that, this understanding of the motives of the apostles does not make them responsible for the actions of Christians over the next centuries. Matthew, Mark, Luke, and John could not have seen that their accounts would become sacred and reach a status close to that of divinity. There is no need to rehearse how the Bible, particularly the New Testament, has been used by Christians throughout the centuries to justify everything from the crusades to slavery. Therefore, if later Christians have taken the gospels and used them as tools to justify their acts of violence against Jewish people, it is tempting to lay that at the feet of the gospel writers as well. However it is far more possible that later acts of violence against the Jewish people had more to do with ignorance and fear than religion or ethnicity.

It is unfortunate that historians do not have evidence written by the Jewish religious leaders about these events. Perhaps first century Jewish writers thought that Jesus of Nazareth did not warrant written responses. They simply had their hands full with the Romans and did not have time to deal with Jesus until it became clear that these followers of Jesus of Nazareth were not just another sect of Judaism but were rejecting the Judaism of the rabbis and indeed all other religions as legitimate expressions of a peoples spiritual lives. Hagner, after arguing that the New Testament is anti-Judaic, but not anti-Semitic, writes:

> The problem for many, however, is not simply that the anti-Judaic passages of the New Testament, but the absolute claim of Christianity over all other options, including Judaism. This claim is itself thought to be objectionable because with it seems to come an ecclesiastical triumphalism and imperialism that cannot tolerate the continued existence of Judaism.[94]

So we are left with one side of the story, and it is a side that is not just unflattering to both Judaism and the Jewish people but can also be seen as the groundwork for centuries of hostility and violence that is almost unprecedented.

Notes

1. Rosemary Ruether, *Faith and Fratricide: The Theological Roots of anti-Semitism* (Minneapolis, MN: Seabury Press, 1974), 78.

2. Leon Sheleff, *In the Shadow of the Cross: Jewish-Christian Relations Through the Ages*, (Portland, OR: Vallentine Mitchell, 2004), 57–58.

3. Douglas R. A. Hare, "The Rejection of the Jews in the Synoptic Gospels and Acts," in *AntiSemitism and the Foundations of Christianity*, ed. Alan T. Davies (New York: Paulist Press, 1979), 31–32.

4. Joseph Klausner, *The Messianic Idea in Israel: From its Beginning to the Completion of the Mishnah* (New York: Macmillan Co., 1955), 7.

5. Ibid.

6. Ibid., 35.

7. Ibid., 51.

8. Lillian Freudmann, *Antisemitism in the New Testament* (Lanham, MD: University Press of America, 1994), 22.

9. Jacob Neusner, *Judaism in the Beginning of Christianity* (Philadelphia, PA: Fortress Press, 1984), 13.

10. Freudmann, *Antisemitism in the New Testament*, 21–22.

11. Philip S. Alexander, "The Parting of the Ways' from the Perspective of Rabbinic Judaism," in *Jews and Christians: The Parting of the Ways, A.D. 70 to 135*, ed. James D. G. Dunn (Grand Rapids, MI: William B. Eerdmans Publishing Company, 1992), 19.

12. John C. Meagher, "As the Twig Was Bent: Antisemitism in Greco-Roman and Earliest Christian Times," in *AntiSemitism and the Foundations of Christianity*, ed. Alan T. Davies (New York: Paulist Press, 1979), 15.

13. Sheleff, *In the Shadow of the Cross*, 74.

14. Ibid., 75.

15. Ibid.; quoted in C. H. Dodd, *The Interpretation of the Fourth Gospel* (Cambridge: Cambridge University Press, 1968), 241.

16. I am indebted to The Christian Think Tank, specifically their Web site, http://www.christian-thinktank.com, for much of this information.

17. The Christian Think Tank at http://www.christian-thinktank.com

18. The authors of the Christians Think Tank say that Edersheim counts 352 passages in the Tanakh that are interpreted messianically in the Rabbinical writings.

19. B. M. Boksar, "Messianism, the Exodus Pattern, and Early Rabbinical Judaism," in *The Messiah: Developments in Earliest Judaism and Christianity*, James Charlesworth ed. (Minneapolis, MN: Fortress Press, 1992), 256.

20. John Collins, "Messianism in the Maccabean Period," in *Judaisms and Their Messiahs at the Turn of the Christian Era*, ed. Jacob Neusner, William Scott Green, and Ernest S. Frerichs (New York: Cambridge University Press, 1987), 101.

21. James Charlesworth, ed., *The Messiah: Developments in Earliest Judaism and Christianity* (Minneapolis, MN: Fortress Press, 1992), 7.

22. E. Earle Ellis, "Biblical Interpretation in the New Testament Church," in *Mikra: Text, Translation, Reading and Interpretation of the Hebrew Bible in Ancient Judaism and Early Christianity*, ed. Martin Jan Mulder (Philadelphia, PA: Fortress Press, 1988) 691.

23. Ibid.

24. Gnostic Christians, who valued the teachings of Jesus while rejecting His sacrifice, would have accepted the Q Gospel, but we have no evidence of Gnostic Christianity before the 2nd century.

25. Marcus Borg, *The Lost Q Gospel: The Original Sayings of Jesus* (Berkeley, CA: Ulysses Press, 1996), 127–128.

26. M. A Powell, *Jesus as a Figure in* History (Louisville, KY: Westminster John Knox, 1998), 39–40; quoted in David A. DeSilva, *An Introduction to the New Testament:*

Contexts, Methods, and Ministry Formation (Downers Grove, IL: InterVarsity Press, 2004), 168–169.

27. J. S. Kloppenborg, *Excavating Q: The History and Setting of the Sayings Gospel* (Minneapolis, MN: Fortress Press, 2000), 100; quoted in David A. DeSilva, *An Introduction to the New Testament: Contexts, Methods, and Ministry Formation* (Downers Grove, IL: InterVarsity Press, 2004), 168.

28. See Mt 12.38–45.

29. *Tar. Jon.* on Jer 30.9, 21.

30. Randal Helms, *Gospel Fictions* (Amherst, NY: Prometheus Books, 1988), 44.

31. *Gos. Thom.* 86. All Gnostic texts in this chapter are taken from *The Nag Hammadi Library* edited by James Robinson. The Gospel of Thomas was translated by Thomas A. Lambdin.

32. *Gos. Phil.,* 81. trans. by Wesley W. Isenberg.

33. There never was an official, orthodox statement of what Gnostics believed, and because of this, it would be unwise to assume that all Gnostic believers believed the same thing. Like other Christians, what they believed about a number of things was still in flux.

34. Trans. by Douglas Parrot.

35. Trans. by Douglas Parrot.

36. Trans. by Francis Williams.

37. Trans. by Helmut Koester and Elaine Pagels.

38. Trans. by Dieter Mueller.

39. Trans. by Malcolm Peel.

40. Trans. by Birger Pearson and Soren Giversen.

41. Trans. by James Brashler and Roger Bullard.

42. Trans. by Joseph Gibbons and Roger Bullard.

43. I have chosen to examine these texts in the scholarly accepted chronological order.

44. There are, of course, other passages in the Gospels where Jesus and the religious leaders confront each other, that is, Mt 8, 9, and 23, and while these cannot be dismissed, the primary focus of the hostility between Jesus and the religious leaders are found in the passages where he uses the self-identifying term, "Son of Man."

45. The only non-gospel use of the term is found in Acts 7.56: "[Stephen], being full of the Holy Spirit, gazed into heaven and saw the glory of God, and Jesus standing at the right hand of God, and said, 'Look! I see the heavens opened and the Son of Man standing at the right hand of God!' And they cried out with a loud voice, stopped their ears, and ran at him with one accord."

46. Luke is more likely than Matthew or Mark to include the general populace in the audiences. However, there are passages where Matthew and/or Mark include the populace and Luke does not.

47. It can be noted here that not a few of the Church Fathers, not surprisingly, equated Jesus as the "Son of Man" with Jesus the "Son of God." A few examples are Ambrose, *Exposition of the Christian Faith* 17.138; Augustine, *Handbook on Faith, Hope and Love* 12.40; Hippolytus, *Refutation of All Heresies* 8; John Cassian, *The Incarnation of the Lord Against Nestorius* 4.7; John of Damascus, *An Exact Exposition of the Orthodox Faith* 3.4; Novatian, *Elucidations* 24; Pseudo-Gregory Thaumaturgus, *Twelve Topics on the Faith* 6.

48. The note on v.13 in the NKJV says that Nestle-Aland and the third edition of the United Bible Societies' New Testament omit "who is in heaven."

49. cf. Acts 6.9–7.60. One of the charges brought against Stephen was that he spoke "blasphemous words against Moses (the law?) and God" (6.11).

50. Jerome, *Commentary on Matthew*, 1.9.3.

51. John Chrysostom, *The Gospel of Matthew, Homily 29.2*.

52. v.16 reads, "For this reason the Jews persecuted Jesus, and sought to kill Him, because He had done these things on the Sabbath."

53. John T. Townsend, "The Gospel of John and the Jews: The Story of a Religious Divorce," in *AntiSemitism and the Foundation of Christianity*, ed. Alan Davies (New York: Paulist Press, 1979), 74.

54. Ibid.

55. Ibid.

56. Ibid.

57. This is, of course, only true if John is following, himself, a chronological order of events as he remembers them. If, however, he is writing thematically, that is, grouping stories and sayings together to establish a theme, then an argument for an order of events is of no consequence.

58. Although it is true that some of the Jewish people did not believe in eternal life, clearly many did, for it is a subject that Jesus continually brings up in these two chapters.

59. The audacity of Jesus that Moses, when he was in the presence of God on Mt. Horeb, "hid his face, for he was afraid to look upon God."

60. Cf. Ex 24:16; Ex 40:35, Nu 9:16-18.

61. cf. *The New International Bible*, vol. 8, *Matthew* (Nashville, TN: Abingdon Press, 1995), 285.

62. Emerton, Cranfield, and Stanton, *The International Critical Commentary*, 335.

63. Anonymous, *Ancient Christian Commentary*, 245.

64. Augustine, *Sermon 71.1*.

65. Meagher argues that the gospel preached by two of the disciples of Jesus, Stephen and Paul, "was intolerable . . . not because of its exaltation of Jesus, but because of its trivialization of the Law." Meagher, "As the Twig is Bent," 20-21.

66. Hare, "The Rejection of the Jews in the Synoptic Gospels and Acts," 31-32.

67. Claudia Setzer, *Jewish Reponses to Early Christians: History and Polemics, 30-150 C.E.*, (Minneapolis, MN: Fortress Press, 1994), 12.

68. 1 Ki 10.9: "Blessed be the Lord your God, who delighted in you, sitting you on the throne of Israel! Because the Lord has loved Israel forever, therefore He made you king, to do justice and righteousness."

69. Theodore of Mopsuestia, *Fragment 74*.

70. It is important to note that all three synoptic gospels carry this story, which means that it was most likely not found in the Q gospel.

71. There is a strong possibility it came from Mark.

72. Epiphanius the Latin, *Interpretation of the Gospels* 28.

73. Ibid.

74. Chrysostom, *The Gospel of Matthew*, Homily 54.1.

75. Theodore of Heraclea, *Fragment 101*.

76. Three additional texts, Mt 17.22–23; Mt 26.1–2; and Lk 18.31–33, demonstrate a foreknowledge by Jesus of his fate. Additionally, the text in Luke introduces the Romans as players in the crucifixion: "Then [Jesus] took the twelve aside and said, 'We are going to Jerusalem, and all things that are written by the prophets concerning the Son of Man will be accomplished. For He will be delivered to the Gentiles and will be mocked and insulted and spit upon. And they will scourge Him and put Him to death.'"

77. That this was not the only accepted soteriological model in the early church is well documented in many works. However, it was a dominant soteriology.

78. Luke's passage is parallel to Matthew's and Mark's, but the term "Son of Man" does not appear in Luke's account.

79. C. Evans writes, "Scribal interpretation is probably based on Mal 4.5–6 . . . which in part reads, 'Behold, I will send you Elijah the prophet *before* the great and terrible day of the Lord comes. And he will turn (LXX: restore) the heart of the father to the son. . . . Belief that Elijah would come at the end of days is attested in a variety of Jewish sources (e.g., Sir 48.10; 4Q558 [4QVision]; *Mek.* On Exod16.33 . . . cf. 1 Macc 14.41. In some texts, Elijah is expected to play a role in the resurrection (*Sib. Or.* 2.187–188; *m. Sofa* 9.15; *b. Sanh.* 113a). The scribes' question probably originated as a challenge to Jesus' proclamation of the kingdom of God. How can Jesus be right if Elijah has not yet made an appearance? We know Elijah must come first. C. Evans, *Word Biblical Commentary*, vol. 34B (Nashville: Thomas Nelson Publishers, 2001), 43.

80. Thayer says that this word is a "*num igitur*, that is marking an inferential question to which a negative answer is expected: Lk. Xviii.8." Joseph Henry Thayer, trans. *A Greek-English Lexicon of the New Testament* (Grand Rapids, MI: Zondervan Publishing House, 1889), 71.

81. Ibid., 474, 475.

82. *Incomplete Work on Matthew*, Homily 33.

83. Cf. Thayer, *A Greek-English Lexicon*, 384.

84. Townsend points out that while "in the *Synoptic Gospels* . . . it is the crowd that cries out against Jesus . . . in John the Jewish presence at the trial is limited to the chief priests and their officers (19.6)." Townsend, "The Gospel of John and the Jews," 77.

85. Paul repeats this curse on the Jews who "opposed him and blasphemed" in Acts 18.4-6. Following their rejection of his testimony "to the Jews that Jesus is the Christ," Paul says, "Your blood be on your own heads; I am clean."

86. Origen, *Commentary on Matthew*, 110.

87. Jerome, *Commentary on Matthew*, 4.26.63.

88. Leo the Great, *Sermon* 44.2.

89. Cyril of Alexandria, *Fragment* 301.

90. Chrysostom, *The Gospel of Matthew*, Homily 85.1.

91. It needs to be noted here that whatever the Jewish people understood "the Holy Spirit" was, it was not part of a divine Godhead. Most observant first century Jews were strict monotheists.

92. Thayer says that the Hebrew equivalent of this word means "the price for redeeming, ransom (paid for slaves, Lev. xix.20; for captives, Is xlv.13; for the ransom of a life, Ex xxi.30; Num xxxv.31," and coupled with ἀντὶ πολλῶν means "to liberate many from the misery and penalty of their sins." Thayer, 384.

93. Ibid., 647.

94. Donald A. Hagner, "Paul's Quarrel with Judaism," in *Anti-Semitism and Early Christianity: Issues of Polemic and Faith*, ed. Craig A. Evans and Donald A. Hagner (Minneapolis, MN: Fortress Press, 1993), 129–130.

Chapter 2
Conflict in the Book of Acts and the Canonical Epistles

It can be argued that the writers of the book of Acts and the canonical epistles were in some ways preoccupied with the Jewish religion and the Jewish people. Many, if not most, of the stories recorded in Acts take place in and around the Temple in Jerusalem or in the synagogues, both in Palestine and in the Diaspora. Common people, King Agrippa, religious leaders, women and children, supporters and detractors, rich and poor are seen or heard in the stories from ch.2–28.

However, more particularly, the authors of Acts were preoccupied with the ultimate fate of the "former" chosen people of God. These Christians spent a great deal of time writing about both the condemnation and salvation of Israel, and the emerging, recognizable, theological context for most of the discussions concerning the Jewish people was the crucifixion of Jesus, more particularly the part the Jewish people played in the crucifixion of Jesus. The charge of deicide is heard early and often. An examination of those texts in Acts will be found in Chapter 3 of this book. However, in the book of Acts and in the Epistles, a picture emerges that suggests that, even when charges of deicide were not thrown into the mix, it was almost impossible for the Jewish people and the Christians to come into contact with each other without it erupting into something more. What follows then are the evidences of what might be called "extra-deicide" conflicts between the Jewish people and the Christians in Palestine and beyond.

The Book of Acts

The book of Acts is not immune from the lower and higher critical tools used to examine other New Testament texts, and Freudmann reminds us that "many scholars" do not consider the book of Acts a "reliable historical document."[1] However, as it is a part of the Christian canon, it deserves the same careful analysis regarding some of the earliest Christian attitudes toward the Jewish people as the Gospels. Indeed, the Book of Acts may have been penned before some of the canonical Gospels. We begin with two stories that recount Jewish attempts to silence some of the earliest Christian leaders.

"The Jews" in Acts

> Saul increased all the more in strength, and confounded *the Jews* who dwelt in Damascus, proving that this Jesus is the Christ. Now after many days were past, *the Jews* plotted to kill him . . . Saul had come to Jerusalem . . . and he spoke boldly in the name of the Lord Jesus and disputed against the Hellenists, but they attempted to kill him. (Acts 9.22–23, 27, 29)

> Now about that time Herod the king stretched out his hand to harass some from the church. Then he killed James the brother of John with the sword. And because he saw that it pleased *the Jews*, he proceeded further to seize Peter also. (Acts 12.1–3a)

The synoptic gospel writers, in an overwhelming majority of the texts, provide the readers with the names of the groups of people who are opposing Jesus. They are either Pharisees, Sadducees, the High Priest, priests, lawyers, and/or scribes, and these groups are portrayed as working either alone or in tandem against Jesus and His apostles. However, in the book of Acts (as in the Gospel of John), again in an overwhelming majority of the texts, the opposition to the followers of Jesus are simply identified as "the Jews."[2] There are a number of ways of understanding this change.

A) The author of Acts prefers to group together linguistically all Jewish opposition as "the Jews," without specific identification as to their sect or status.

B) The Jewish opposition has grown to the point at which many more of the common people, without any specific sect allegiance, have joined the groups identified in the synoptic gospels in their opposition to Jesus and his followers.

C) The third possibility is the most troubling. The author of the book of Acts may be suggesting to the readers and hearers of his stories that it is no longer the religious leaders who are guilty of spiritual blindness and resistant to the call of God. All of the Jewish people have now been given the pejorative label "the Jews." Throughout the book of Acts it is "the Jews" who either plot the death of the followers of Jesus or provide evidence against them when they are brought before the Roman authorities to answer questions of sedition.

If this third interpretation is accepted, then it was less than difficult for the early Church Fathers to take the next accusatory step *viz.*, if *all* of "the Jews" of that age are guilty of resistance to God, and rejection of His Messiah, then it is possible that *all* Jews, at all times, both past and future, in all places, are also guilty of the same sins. These interpreters argue, in a gross misinterpretation, that the Tanakh itself provides ample evidence that the ancient Hebrews, Israelites, and Jews could not be faithful to God for more than a few generations. Both the major and minor prophets are full of warnings and threats from God for waywardness. A few of the Jewish heroes mentioned in the Tanakh were able to escape these sins, but the evidence now, according to these early post-crucifixion, Christian exegetes of the Tanakh, is that most did not. What that conclusion, then, translates to will be discussed in subsequent chapters, but the use of term "the Jews" by Christians as a pejorative term may have begun here in the book of Acts.

Charges of Blasphemy in Acts

> And the next Sabbath almost the whole city came together to hear the word of God. But when the Jews saw the multitudes, they were filled with envy; and contradicting and blaspheming, they opposed the things spoken by Paul. Then Paul and Barnabas grew bold and said, "It was necessary that the word of God should be spoken to you first; but since you reject it, and judge yourselves unworthy of everlasting life, behold we turn to the Gentiles." . . . But the Jews stirred up the devout and prominent women and the chief men of the city, raised up persecution against Paul and Barnabas, and expelled them from their region. (Acts 13.44–46, 50)

The charges of "blasphemy" brought against Jesus in both the synoptic gospels (Mt 9.3, 26.65, Mk 14.64), and the Gospel of John (10.33–36), have now, in Acts, been turned on the Jewish people.[3] The text of Acts 13 does not reveal what Paul was preaching other than the rather vague term "the word of God." Whether this was a reference to the already accepted authority of the Tanakh as the word of God, or whether the author of Acts is beginning to use this term to include specific Christian teachings and preaching about and by Jesus, is not made known. In comparison, the charge brought against Stephen in Acts 7.11 of speaking "blasphemous words against Moses and God" suggests that at least the Torah was being used as sacred and holy.

It can be assumed that Paul was either preaching or teaching about Jesus. Whether he was simply telling the story of Jesus or explaining what the life and death of Jesus meant, or whether he was, as early Christians often did, using the Tanakh to argue that Jesus was the fulfillment of the prophesies, it was enough to cause opposition from the Jewish people, and that opposition was seen by the Christians as blasphemy.

Charges of Jewish blasphemy are also heard in Acts 18 where Paul, with Silas and Timothy, in the synagogue in Corinth, "testified to the Jews that Jesus is the Christ." The text then reads that the Jews "opposed him and blasphemed" (v.6).

Whatever Paul's message was, these stories are early examples of a tactic early Christians used against all of their enemies, but especially against the Jewish people, taking the weapons aimed at them, and turning them around to use against their enemies. "It was not Jesus who was guilty of blasphemy against God, but you who are guilty of blasphemy against God. And because your opposition comes against not just me (in this case Paul), but against the "word of God" I am proclaiming, your sin is even worse."

The Canonical Epistles

The Case of the Apostle Paul

The Apostle Paul, either justly or unjustly, has received as much criticism as the Apostles Matthew and John for the developing divide between first century Judaism and first century Christianity. Therefore, those interested in early Christian precedents for hostility toward Judaism and the Jewish people cannot ignore the Pauline Epistles.

The number of scholars who have turned their attention to Paul's part in the separation between Judaism and Christianity, both Jewish and Christian, continues to grow, and the theories which attempt to explain Paul's part in this estrangement are as numerous as the scholars.[4] Therefore, it is not my intention to rehearse all of the opinions voiced to date but to rely on those who have refused to stake out what may be considered extreme positions.

Bruce Chilton writes that a "plausible hypothesis" for the growing estrangement begins with the assumption that "Jesus and his movement initially were essentially Judaic."[5] While this is certainly not difficult to defend, he goes on to say that "the changing constituencies of the church over time—particularly reflected in the Pauline corpus—transformed the movement into a systematic alternative to the rabbinic Judaism that emerged after 70 C.E."[6] I would argue that while Jesus saw himself first and foremost as a Jew, it was his understanding of who he was, that is, Messiah, Son of Man, Son of God, and what he understood true Judaism to be that began the separation. Secondly, early to mid-first century Christians, the accepted time of the flourishing of the Apostle Paul, were not able to systematize their own beliefs, let alone develop a systematic response to Judaism. That would come much later, but the architects of that system certainly used the gospels and the letters of Paul as underpinnings.

Donald Hagner sees Paul arguing against what he perceived to be a "truncated version" of Judaism, and that Christianity was simply "the fulfillment of Judaism."[7] He supports his argument by quoting the Jewish scholar Hans Joachim Schoeps who wrote, "Paul is in fact convinced that he has never seceded from Judaism, since the Christian confession means for him the completion of the Jewish faith."[8] However, one cannot read 1 Thess 2.14–16 and believe that Paul's argument with the Jewish people is purely philosophical or even theological. In an effort to extricate Paul from charges of anti-Semitism, Hagner says that Paul's words here are evidence of his anti-Judaism, not anti-Semitism.[9]

Paul's Preaching in Acts

The Jewish Targets of Paul's Preaching in Acts. The Apostle Paul is often called the "Apostle to the Gentiles." However, in Acts 9.15, Ananias is told by God that Paul is a "chosen vessel of Mine to bear my name before Gentiles, kings, *and the children of Israel*" (emphasis added). Further, in the chronicling of Paul's evangelistic missions in the book of Acts, it is to the Jewish synagogues of the various cities that he first turns his attention. It leaves one to wonder why the man considered as one of the greatest apostles would be given a title that would suggest that he was an apostle to the Gentiles and not the Jewish people. Is it possible that the Jewish people were not seen as worthy of the work of one who is considered by some as the greatest apostle and even the founder of Christianity? Further, those attempting to argue that Paul is the Apostle to the Gentiles because of his letters to *Christians* in the various cities, have forgotten that many of these churches were populated with both Jewish and Gentile believers.

For example, first century Damascus must have had a sizeable enough Jewish population to support more then one synagogue, for Acts 9 says that Paul "preached the Christ in the synagogues; that He is the Son of God" (v.20). Apparently Paul was allowed to preach in these synagogues more then once, for he "increased all the more in strength, and confounded the Jews who dwelt in Damascus, proving that this Jesus is the Christ," and it was only after some time that "the Jews plotted to kill him" (v.23). There is no evidence that in Damascus Paul attempted to preach his gospel to a purely Gentile audience.

In Acts 13, we read that the Holy Spirit, speaking to several Christian prophets and teachers, says, "Now separate to Me Barnabas and Saul (Paul) for the work to which I have called them" (v.2). In v.5, that "work" is revealed. Paul, Barnabas, and John Mark, after going through Seleucia and Cyprus, began to preach "the word of God in the synagogues of the Jews in Salamis." Here, again, there is evidence of more than one synagogue, and Paul and his associates are allowed to preach in more than one of them. If the preaching at the synagogues of Salamis was not a random stop in the itinerary of Paul and his companions but a response to their understanding to where the Holy Spirit was directing them, then this event can be interpreted as evidence that either God and/or the early Christians saw the Jewish believers as people worthy of the efforts of the apostles and disciples of Jesus to evangelize them. Further, it cannot be argued that Paul simply went to these synagogues to condemn the Jewish leaders in Jerusalem for killing Jesus. No text of Paul's sermons exist. It can be assumed that God would not direct these men to engage their time and efforts to a people who they believed God had already abandoned and rejected. In other words, Paul's preaching in the Mediterranean synagogues was his obedient response to the command of the Holy Spirit. If that is so, then some conclusions about how quickly early Christians saw the Jewish people as "others," or "them," may need to be revaluated.

Notice the following:

A) Acts 9.20:
1) Damascus
2) Paul
3) Following his conversion and healing from the divinely imposed three-day blindness, Paul "immediately . . . preached the Christ in the synagogues, that He is the Son of God."

B) Acts 13.5:
1) Salamis
2) Paul, Barnabas, and John Mark
3) See comments above.

C) Acts 13.13–43:
1) Antioch in Pisidia
2) Paul and his party
3) The text of Paul's sermon is recorded in the "synagogue on the Sabbath day" (v.14). At the conclusion of the sermon, "many of the Jews and devout proselytes followed Paul and Barnabas, who, speaking to them, persuaded them to continue in the grace of God" (v.43).

D) Acts 14.1:
1) Iconium
2) Paul and Barnabas
3) On arriving at Iconium, Paul and Barnabas "went together to the synagogue of the Jews, and so spoke that a great multitude both of the Jews and of the Greeks believed." Verse 3 says that they "stayed there a long time," but whether they continued to preach in the synagogue is uncertain. The evidence suggests that they did not.

E) Acts 17.1–4:
1) Thessalonica
2) Paul and Silas
3) Paul and Silas "came to Thessalonica, where there was a synagogue of the Jews. Then Paul, *as his custom was*, went in to them, and for three Sabbaths reasoned with them from the Scriptures, explaining and demonstrating that the Christ had to suffer and rise again from the dead, and saying, 'This Jesus whom I preach to you is the Christ.' And some of them were persuaded; and a great multitude of the devout Greeks, and not a few of the leading women, joined Paul and Silas" (emphasis added).

F) Acts 17.10–12:
1) Berea
2) Paul and Silas
3) "When [Paul and Silas] arrived [in Berea] they went into the synagogue of the Jews. These [worshipers at the synagogue] received the word with all readiness. . . . Therefore many of them believed, and also not a few of the Greeks, prominent women as well as men."

G) Acts 17.17:
1) Athens
2) Paul
3) Although the speech of Paul on Mars Hill is the story most remembered from his visit to Athens, the text says that, as he waited for the arrival of Silas and Timothy, "he reasoned in the synagogue with the Jews and with the Gentile worshipers."[10]

H) Acts 18.4–5:
1) Corinth
2) Paul, Silas, and Timothy
3) Staying with Aquila and Priscilla, Paul "reasoned in the synagogue every Sabbath, and persuaded both Jews and Greeks . . . that Jesus is the Christ." How long Paul stayed in Corinth is not told, but reasoning in the synagogue "every Sabbath" suggests that it was more than a few times. Also of interest are Paul's words to the Jews who "opposed him." He says to them, "Your blood be upon your own heads; I am clean. From now on I will go to the Gentiles" (v.6). However, following this episode, Paul is found preaching in the synagogues in Ephesus twice; the second time for three months (Acts 18, 19).

I) Acts 18.19:
1) Ephesus
2) Paul
3) Paul, on his return trip to Antioch, "came to Ephesus [and] entered the synagogue and reasoned with the Jews."

J) Acts 19.8:
1) Ephesus
2) Paul
3) After baptizing new believers who had previously received the "baptism of repentance" from John (the Baptist?), Paul "went into the synagogue and spoke boldly for three months, reasoning and persuading concerning the things of the kingdom of God."

Therefore, while the Apostle Paul may continue to be named the "Apostle to the Gentiles,"[11] in ten different cities, the first place he and his companions preached was in a synagogue or synagogues. This cannot be ignored, and one of the conclusions that can be extrapolated from this evidence is that Paul and those who traveled with him had not, at this time, perceived the Jewish people as unresponsive or unreceptive to his gospel. If the Pauline party believed that God had rejected the Jewish people because of what they perceived as the wrong treatment of Jesus at the hands of the Jewish people, it seems that these early Christians would not have bothered to preach their gospel in the places where the Jewish people worshiped. If they wanted to only reach the Gentiles, they could have gone to the various market places and preached. But in Pisidia, Iconium, Thessalonica, Berea, Athens, and Corinth Paul chose to preach where there were both Jews and Greeks, and the evidence is that both Jews and Greeks responded to the preaching of the disciples. Finally, just because Paul may have discontinued preaching in the Jewish synagogues does not mean that all Christians stopped going to synagogues. The Easter sermons of John Chrysostom in 387 C.E. give ample evidence of the continued presence of Christians worshiping in Jewish synagogues.

The Jewish Reactions to Paul's Preaching in Acts. The author of Acts seems intent on demonstrating that the preaching of the apostles was effective both with the Gentiles and the Jews. Ruether understands Paul to be saying, "In respect to righteousness, there is no difference between circumcision and uncircumcision. Both Jew and Gentile are sold under the power of sin, [and now] salvation comes only through a new covenant founded on the risen Christ."[12] If the accounts can be believed, then, hundreds of Jews, both Palestinian and Diasporic were converted to the new religion. Setzer points out that in Acts 2.41, 2.47, 4.4, 8.5–12, 14.1–7, 17.1–9, 17.10–12, 18.4, 18.7–8, 18.19–20, and 21.20, a percentage of the Jewish people who heard the preaching and/or teaching of the apostles either

    A) gathered to hear,
    B) believed,
    C) were persuaded, or
    D) were baptized.[13]

If the author of Acts is to believed, in Jerusalem, the very heart of Judaism, 3,000 (2.41) and 5,000 (4.4) are baptized at different times, and by the time of Acts 21.20, the number of Jewish believers are "myriads" (Gr = $\mu\nu\rho\iota\acute{\alpha}\delta\epsilon\varsigma$; lit = an innumerable number; an unlimited number[14]).

However, not all were converted, and the reception of the preaching of Paul and the other disciples was mixed. There was also almost constant resistance, and the rest of the stories in Acts that speak to the conflict with the Jewish people and the Apostles, principally Paul, are variations of attempts either to silence the Apostles or kill them. Examples are Acts 13.50, which says that "the Jews stirred up the devout and prominent women and the chief men of the city, raised up persecution against Paul and Barnabas, and expelled them from their region." In Iconium, "the unbelieving Jews stirred up the Gentiles and poisoned their minds against the brethren" (ch.14.2). In Thessalonica, "the Jews, . . . becoming envious, took some of the evil men from the marketplace, and gathering a mob, set all the city in an uproar" (ch.17.5).

It also seems that groups of Jewish men took it upon themselves to follow Paul and the Apostles for the purpose of opposing them. While at Lystra, "Jews from Antioch and Iconium came there; and having persuaded the multitudes, they stoned Paul and dragged him out of the city, supposing him to de dead" (ch.14.19). Crowds in Berea were stirred up against Paul and Silas by Jews who came from Thessalonica (ch.17.13). Finally, in Jerusalem, "Jews from Asia, seeing [Paul] in the temple, stirred up the whole crowd and laid hands on him" (ch.21.27).

Paul's Attempt to Rewrite Israel's History

> Moses ... put a veil over his face so that the children of Israel could not look steadily at the end of what was passing away (Gr = τό τέλος τοῦ καταργουμένου; lit = "the end of the thing fading away"). But their minds were hardened. For until this day the same veil remains unlifted in the reading of the Old Testament, because the veil is taken away in Christ. But even to this day, when Moses is read, a veil lies on their heart. (2 Cor 3.13–15)

> You who make your boast in the law, do you dishonor God through breaking the law? For *'The name of God is blasphemed among the Gentiles because of you,'* as it is written. (Rom 2.23–24)

> Israel, pursuing the law of righteousness, has not attained to the law of righteousness. Why? Because they did not seek it by faith, but as it were, by the works of the law. For they stumbled at the stumbling stone. (Rom 9.31–32)

> For I bear [the Jewish people] witness that they have a zeal for God, but not according to knowledge (Gr = ἐπίγνωσιν). For they being ignorant (Gr = ἀγνοοῦντες) of God's righteousness, and seeking to establish their own righteousness, have not submitted to the righteousness of God. For Christ is the end of the law for righteousness to everyone who believes. (Rom 10.2–4)

These texts are early examples of a favorite accusation of early Christian authors, that is, the Jewish people never understood God or God's word in the past, and this spiritual blindness remains to the present day, for the true spiritual understanding of God's word comes through an acceptance of Jesus Christ. This is an interpretation of these texts that is especially egregious, polemical, and problematic. Telling a people that they have lived under a self-imposed ignorance of their own divinely given sacred scriptures is telling them that their history, religion, culture is based on an ignorance of God and God's purposes for them. In other words, their whole existence as a people is based on lies and misunderstanding. Further, this interpretation says to the Jewish people that they cannot retrieve that history; that it will always be a part of their legacy, and that they will continue to live in darkness and ignorance until they accept what God, their God, has done through Jesus Christ. However, that interpretation ignores what Hare calls "prophetic anti-Judaism," which he describes as a "hallowed tradition in Israel" where "it is common place for the prophets to accuse priests and teachers of the Torah, including other prophets, of special responsibility for Israel's apostasy."[15] He suggests that Paul is following this tradition, for he goes on to say, "Jewish-Christian anti-Judaism retained the basic assumption of prophetic anti-Judaism that repentance was possible because God had not rejected his people."[16]

The overwhelming reaction to this accusation from the Jewish populations cannot have been favorable. One can imagine how Christians would react to a powerful message from a group claiming to be the true Christianity telling the rest of Christians that they have constantly misunderstood the word of God, and that because of that misunderstanding, they have relinquished any right to be called followers of God. Yet this is an oft-repeated scenario in the history of Christianity itself, with each new expression of Christianity often telling the "mother church" that they have either never understood the word of God or that they have been led to false understandings, and are, therefore, no longer to be considered true followers of the true God.

Therefore, while many faithful Jewish believers, like all religious people, would have been aware of a lack of true expressions of their religion, even by some of their religious leaders, to have other Jewish believers condemn their entire religious and spiritual history would have been unacceptable and would produced a reaction of rejection and opposition. To be accused of spiritual blindness is not often met with open arms, and it is this attitude by the Christians that would exacerbate a separation that would only continue until both sides reach a point where they are unable to speak with each other without rancor and suspicion.

One might conclude that what we have from Paul here is an ethos of condescension and perhaps even pity if we imagine him saying, "If the poor benighted Jews would only accept what God has given, they can continue to be a part of God's chosen people. But as it stands now, most have neither the ability nor knowledge to make that decision, and will ultimately suffer for their ignorance and unbelief."

However, the ethos between the early Christians and Jewish people who chose not to believe that Jesus of Nazareth was the promised Messiah is much more nuanced than what is found in these few verses. These early Christians were still piecing together an understanding of the meaning of the life, death, and resurrection of Jesus themselves. Issues of grace, justification and righteousness, salvation, and the efficaciousness of the crucifixion did not come fully articulated to them from God. Their understandings of these and other issues were a work in progress.

Notes

1. Lillian C. Freudmann, *AntiSemitism in the New Testament* (Lanham, MD: University Press of America, 1994), 101.

2. See footnote 7 in "Introduction."

3. John Townsend argues that "whereas the other gospels insist that the charges against Jesus were blasphemy, John 11.48 makes it clear that the Jewish authorities were concerned lest Jesus disrupt political relations with Rome." John C. Townsend, "The Gospel of John and the Jews: The Story of a Religious Divorce," in *Antisemitism and the Foundation of Christianity*, ed. Alan Davies (New York: Paulist Press, 1979), 76.

4. cf. Bibliography at the end of this book.

5. Bruce Chilton, "Jesus and the Question of Anti-Semitism," in *Anti-Semitism and Early Christianity: Issues of Polemic and Faith*, ed. Craig A. Evans and Donald A. Hagner (Minneapolis, MN: Fortress Press, 1993), 42.

6. Ibid.

7. Donald A. Hagner, "Paul's Quarrel with Judaism," in *Anti-Semitism and Early Christianity: Issues of Polemic and Faith*, ed. Craig A. Evans and Donald A. Hagner (Minneapolis, MN: Fortress Press, 1993), 129.

8. Ibid., 150. See H. J. Schoeps, *Paul: The Theology of the Apostle in the Light of Jewish Religious History*, trans. H. Knight (Philadelphia, Pa: Westminster Press, 1961), 234.

9. Ibid., 130.

10 While Paul preached in the other towns, when he comes to Athens, the ancient seat of philosophy, logic and reason, Paul "reasons" in the synagogue. Also, after this experience in Athens, Paul is also described as reasoning in Corinth and Ephesus.

11. See Acts 9.15: "But the Lord said to [Ananias], 'Go, for [Saul] is a chosen vessel of Mine to bear My name before Gentiles." And Gal 2.7: "When [the Apostles in Jerusalem] saw that the gospel for the uncircumcised had been committed to me, as the gospel for the circumcised was to Peter."

12. Rosemary Radford Ruether, *Faith and Fratricide: The Theological Roots of Anti-Semitism* (Minneapolis, MN: Seabury Press, 1974), 97.

13. Claudia Setzer, *Jewish Responses to Early Christians: History and Polemics, 30-150 C.E.* (Minneapolis, MN: Fortress Press, 1994), 48–51.

14. Joseph Henry Thayer, trans. *A Greek-English Lexicon of the New Testament* (Grand Rapids, MI: Zondervan Publishing House, 1889), 419.

15. Douglas R. A. Hare, "The Rejection of the Jews in the Synoptic Gospels and Acts," in *AntiSemitism and the Foundations of Christianity*, ed. Alan T. Davies (New York: Paulist Press, 1979), 29.

16. Ibid., 30.

Chapter 3
Deicide, Divine Predetermination, and Deliverance in the New Testament

One of the most damning accusations made against the Jewish people was the charge of deicide; a charge that has been used for centuries as justification for brutality and inhumanity on unprecedented scales. It is a charge that has both a long and ancient pedigree, and one that has had inconceivable consequences. Marvin Perry and Frederick M. Schweitzer, with brutal clarity, write,

> In the gospels' rendition [of the crucifixion of Jesus] and as interpreted for centuries, the Jews are perceived as "the Christ killers," a people condemned forever to suffer exile and degradation. This archcrime of "deicide," of murdering God, turned the Jews into the embodiment of evil, a "criminal people" cursed by God and doomed to wander and suffer tribulation to the end of time. No other religious tradition has condemned a people as the murderers of its god, a unique accusation that has resulted in a unique history of hatred, fear, and persecution. When it came to the Jews, the central doctrine of Christianity, that Jesus was providentially sent into the world to atone by his death for mankind's' sins, was obscured. . . . Ultimately, all anti-Semitic accusations and justifications for persecution and discrimination spring from that primal act of deicide."[1]

They go on to quote John Dominic Crossan, who writes,

The passion-resurrection stories [are] the matrix for Christian anti-Judaism and eventually for European anti-Semitism" [and] that "without that Christian anti-Judaism, lethal and genocidal European antisemitism would have been either impossible or at least not widely successful.[2]

Most, though not all, early Christians believed Jesus Christ to be God incarnate, come to this world to save it and His followers (Jhn 3.16).[3] However, even though many were taught that His death on the cross was preordained by Him and His Father, the animosity toward the people who they believed actually carried out the crucifixion (the Jews sans the Romans), led the followers of Jesus to believe that these people (the Jews) were guilty of the worst sort of crime; a crime against the world and a crime against divinity. Though no non-Christians and most Christians never fully worked out the theological complexities of the idea of the Christian trinity, it was believed that there was one God, and Jesus was the human manifestation of that one God, and to kill Him on the hated cross was not something the early Christians were ready to forgive or, as it turns out, forget.[4]

From non-canonical sources, this charge is heard as early as the second century from Melito of Sardis in his *On Pascha*. However, the question of New Testament antecedents of this charge needs to be addressed. In other words, did the early Church Fathers who charged the Jewish people with deicide invent this charge on their own, or did they, as they did with many theological questions, look for precedents in what they considered their sacred Scriptures? The answer(s) to that question lie in the gospels and epistles.

Sacred Texts and the Charge of Deicide

To begin an exploration of the consequences of interpretations of these texts from the Christians' "word of God" on subsequent Christian/Jewish relations requires a brief excursion into how the early apostles, disciples, and followers of Jesus understood "the word of God."

It is of critical importance to remember that three of the four attributed, canonical, gospel writers are Jewish; Luke being the exception. The Jewish authors, raised in the culture of first century Judaism, would have been trained to believe that the Tanakh contained the truth about their own history, the history of God's dealings with His chosen people, and His dealings with others. The Tanakh was the Word of God.[5] Therefore, it would not be difficult, especially for the early Jewish Christians, to believe the writings of the Apostles of Jesus Christ,[6] their incarnate God, to also be the word of God, and, like the authors of the Tanakh, the carriers of divine truths.

In the first three centuries of the Common era, as different gospel accounts vied for recognition and as different epistles gained and lost acceptance, a religious and theological culture was being formed among the Christians; a religious and theological culture that pitted Christian writings against each other.[7] As early as the second century, competing lists of accepted "Scripture" began to appear.[8] The end result of this competition was a culture that believed that what "we" accept as truth means that anything different "you" accept is false (read "heretical").[9] Therefore, the questions "What is Scripture?" and "What is not Scripture?" became questions of contention among early Christians. What was believed to be "truth," eventually came to mean that what was believed was "righteous." Therefore, if Matthew, Mark, Luke, and John (Matthew and John being eyewitness accounts), in their righteous,[10] authoritative, scriptural,[11] writings say that the Jewish people are responsible for the death of their Savior, then the Jewish people are guilty of killing the Christian God. This is, of course, an oversimplification of a process that took decades to develop, but if early Christian historians are correct in believing that most of the early Christians were not from the educated segment of society (which was itself miniscule), then these early Christians are not going to have the intellectual or theological sophistication to work through the theological subtleties that are attendant with questions of deicide. Further, not only were complete, standard copies of the gospel accounts not readily available to all congregations, but the leaders of these congregations could and did choose which passages in the new "Word of God' to present to their congregations. It is likely that the crucifixion of Jesus was a central teaching theologically, soteriologically, and liturgically, and we can, therefore, assume that the early Christians were fed a steady diet of the accounts of the crucifixion.[12] Further, without any explanation of the context, and with a predisposition to fix blame on the Jews, it is not surprising that early Christians, both educated and non-educated, developed an animosity toward Jewish people. This is not an excuse for the growing estrangement between Christians and Jews, but a partial explanation.[13]

The Charge of Deicide in the Gospels

In the concluding chapter, titled "Crucifixion," in his book *the Shadow of the Cross*, Leon Sheleff aligns himself with Weddig Fricke (and many others) and writes,

> From a practical point of view, there is value in [Fricke's] concluding remark that "the charge of deicide raised against the Jews is historically false, theologically superfluous, and ruinous from a moral point of view."[14]

This quote is preceded by arguments from both Christian and Jewish authors who cast doubt on the veracity of the gospel accounts of the crucifixion and use historical, literary, canonical (both from the Tanakh and the New Testament), and philosophical evidence to support the view that the canonical gospel accounts of the crucifixion of Jesus are examples of revisionist history. And while others have and do present evidence of the veracity of the accounts, most agree that centuries of Christian interpretations of Matthew, Mark, Luke, and John have been ruinous to the Jewish people in terms of their place in history, in terms of their survival in dominant cultures, most notably Christian, and in Jewish/Christian relations.

A reading of the synoptic gospels and the gospel of John reveals a belief by the authors of these gospels that the plot to kill Jesus began early (Jhn 5.18) and continued to the days just preceding the actual crucifixion (Mt 26.2-4). The gospel accounts put the language about killing Jesus in the mouths of the religious leaders (Jhn 5.18; Jhn 11.47-53; Mt 26.2-4; [cf. Mk 14.1, 2; Lk 22.1, 2]), in the mouth of Jesus himself (Jhn 7.19-20, 25; Jhn 8.37, 40; Mt 20.18-19 [cf. Mk 10.32-34]; Lk 18.31-34; Mt 26.2-4 [cf. Mk 14.1, 2]; Lk 22.1, 2), in the mouths of the common people (Jhn 7.19-20, 25), and the writers' own understandings of the events leading up to the crucifixion as they look back on them (Jhn 5.18, 7.1). Therefore, the gospel accounts present stories of the crucifixion that was the culmination of years of plotting by the religious leaders to silence Jesus. Further, Mt 27.22-25 (cf. Mk 15.6-14; Lk 23.17-23; Jhn 18.39, 40) and Jhn 19.14-16a can be read as attempts to both place the blame for the crucifixion solely on the shoulders of the Jewish leaders and people and exonerate the Roman official Pilate. Leon Sheleff writes,

> Over the years, the Jewish people have borne the brunt of the message ensconced in the existence of the Cross: not the Romans, but the Jews bear responsibility for the suffering imposed on the Messiah, the son of God.[15]

In the synoptic account, Pilate literally (and symbolically) washes his hands of the affair while the crowd cries, "His blood be on us and on our children" (Mt 27.25).[16] In the Johanine account, Pilate presents Jesus to the crowd, and they cry, "Away with Him, away with Him! Crucify Him! [and] We have no king but Caesar!" (Jhn 18.15). Yet as Sheleff points out, the "Jews never practiced crucifixion," and he believes that the Jewish people would not conduct such a trail "at a time so close to the Jewish Sabbath and the festival of Passover."[17]

The Charge of Deicide in Acts

The Book of Acts is filled with conflicts between the earliest Christians (principally the Apostles) and the Jewish people, and if the Book of Acts is a faithful account of the experiences of these earliest Christians, then the repeated charges of the unjust murder of Jesus bear testimony of the degree of sorrow, grief, rage, and resentment felt by the Apostles. The accounts of the rising degree of hostility between Jesus and religious leaders in the Gospels, bursting open into what the Christians considered a cataclysmic catastrophe at the crucifixion, and the Book of Acts, written before C.E. 62, lets us know that the wounds were still fresh.[18]

However, there are at least three things that are curious about the charges of deicide and other Jewish/Christian conflicts recorded in the Book of Acts. First, if the tradition of the Lukan authorship of Acts is correct, then the recording of the charge of deicide comes from a non-witness to the crucifixion, and it comes from a non-Jewish author. However, not all scholars agree on the Lukan authorship of Acts, specifically concerning the picture presented of the apostle Paul.

John Gager writing about "Paul's Friends and Enemies" in his book *The Origins of Anti-Semitism* says,

> This is not the place to rehearse the lengthy debates concerning the historical accuracy of Luke's picture [of Paul and his activities]. My own view is that there are sound reasons for doubting every element in this picture. At the very least we may agree with the contention that Luke's version of the Jerusalem meeting [between Paul and his supporters, and the apostles] was precisely what Paul was trying to counter in Galatians 2.[19]

Further, if the tradition of Luke being the most pacific (or least hostile toward the Jewish people) of the Gospel writers is correct, he is not likely to create stories about the conflicts between the Apostles and the Jews to exacerbate further an already extremely tense situation between the Jewish people and the earliest Christians, who were already looking at each other with a great deal of suspicion. This, then, can lead to the conclusion that by the time the book of Acts was penned, the view of the Jewish people being "Christ killers" was already a present, and perhaps even common, theme among Christians. Luke, in the Book of Acts, then, is either faithfully reflecting what he is witnessing, or the author of Acts is purposefully fueling the animosity between the Christians and the Jewish people.

Second, traditionally the Apostles Paul, Matthew, and John, have been viewed as the principle authors of New Testament antipathy and hostility toward first century Judaism. Gager notes that this reputation, in part, is attributable to those early Christian authors who, wishing to claim orthodoxy, wrote in Paul's name. And even though modern scholars have rejected all of the non-canonical and a few of the canonical writings claiming a Pauling authorship, the "most thoroughgoing and systematic repudiation of Judaism in early Christianity was articulated under the banner of Pauline authority."[20] In spite of all of that, Paul, in the book of Acts at least, only once (Acts 13.28), reminds the Jewish people of their part in the crucifixion.

The third point is that in the Book of Acts, the author makes it clear that it was not just a good man, or even just a righteous man that the Jewish people killed, but God. However they understood Jesus to be God theologically is less important here than the belief that He was, in some way, God; the God of the Tanakh, and as such, the Jews have killed their own God.

The following, then, is an examination of the texts in Acts where the charge of deicide is heard.

> Men of Israel, hear these words: Jesus of Nazareth, a Man attested by God to you by miracles, wonders, and signs which God did through Him in your midst, as you yourselves also know—Him, being delivered by the determined counsel and foreknowledge of God, you have taken by lawless hands, have crucified, and put to death. (Acts 2.22-23)

In the middle of his sermon on the day of Pentecost, in Jerusalem, with thousands of Jewish people from the Jewish Diaspora listening, Peter charges the "men of Israel" with the death of "a Man attested by God." Seemingly to avoid any misunderstanding among the non-Palestinians in the crowd as to who this "Man attested by God" was, Peter concludes his sermon with these words: "Therefore, let all the house of Israel know assuredly that God has made this Jesus, whom you crucified, both Lord and Christ" (v.36).

The book of Acts, because of its context, is not concerned with the differences of understanding of religious or theological or moral issues between Jesus and the Jewish leaders. Further, it is not just the Jewish leaders who are guilty of the crucifixion, but the wider "men of Israel" are now also complicit in the crime. Peter's quotes from Joel 2.28–32, Ps 16.8–11, and Ps 110.1 are an early example of the Christian's christological interpretation of the Tanakh to damn the Jewish people for their refusal to acknowledge Jesus as the Christ and as God incarnate.[21] The intention of the use of these texts is this: "Not only do we condemn you, but your own sacred Scriptures condemn you." Jesus, more than once, in arguments with the Jewish leaders, accused them of being "mistaken, not knowing the Scriptures nor the power of God" (Mt 22.29).

This use of the Tanakh to condemn the first century Jewish leaders and people has already been heard in the Gospels.[22] It will be heard again in the Epistles[23] and is a favorite tool of the early church Fathers to explain the sorrows that have fallen on the Jewish people since the crucifixion. Tertullian went so far as to declare that none of the enemies of Christianity, Jewish, pagan, or heretical Christians, could use Scriptures to argue with the true Christians, for all Scripture belonged only to the true Christians.

> Men of Israel . . . the God of Abraham, Isaac, and Jacob, the God of our fathers, glorified His Servant Jesus, whom you delivered up and denied in the presence of Pilate, when he was determined to let *Him* go. But you denied the Holy One and the Just, and asked for a murderer to be granted to you, and killed the Prince of life whom God raised from the dead, of which we are witnesses. . . . Yet now, brethren, I know that you did it in ignorance, as did all your rulers. (Acts 3.12–15)

Only once in Acts are "others" indicted in the crucifixion of Jesus. In Acts 4.24–28, Herod, Pontius Pilate, and the Gentiles are included as co-conspirators in the death of Jesus, but even then Herod, Pontius Pilate, and the Gentiles are seen as being submissive to the will of God, for they "were gathered together to do whatever Your hand and Your purpose determined before to be done." Further, in Acts 3, Pilate's determination "to let Him go" can be seen either as an attempt to obviate Pilate's responsibility in the crucifixion altogether, and/or fix the blame on the Jewish leaders alone. Therefore, only the Jews stand condemned.

However, Peter "magnanimously" says, "brethren, I know that you did it in ignorance, as did your rulers." An interpretation of this could read, "You killed the Holy and Just incarnation of God, but you did this because of your ignorance of your own Scriptures. And not only did you not understand the Tanakh's teachings about the coming Messiah, but your rulers, who are students of the Tanakh, were ignorant of its true teachings." Therefore, although Peter may allow the ignorance of the Jewish people to pass, later Christian writers will roundly condemn them for this same "ignorance," often declaring that it was willful ignorance, and therefore all judgments on them from God are justified.

> Then Peter, filled with the Holy Spirit, said to them, "Rulers of the people and elders of Israel . . . let it be known to you all, and to all the people of Israel, that by the name of Jesus Christ of Nazareth whom you crucified, whom God raised from the dead, by Him this man stands here before you whole. This is the *'stone which was rejected by you builders, which has become the chief cornerstone.* (Acts 4.8–11)

The Apostles' belief of the ignorance of both the Jewish people and the leaders of the Jewish people of their own Scriptures is further stated here where Ps 118.22 is given a christological interpretation. Many early Christian writers were eager to demonstrate to other Christians and non-Christians that Jesus was the fulfillment of many of the prophesies found in the Tanakh. Many of the events, people, and rituals found in the Tanakh were seen as "types" of Jesus Christ, who was the great "ante-type." Therefore, if Jesus was the fulfillment of the stories and prophesies from the Tanakh, then the Tanakh itself can be used as a weapon against the original recipients of these writings. In other words, the Tanakh itself condemns the Jewish people for they completely misunderstood its true import. These early Christians believed that because of what happened to Jesus in Jerusalem, on the cross, He has to be the "stone which was rejected by you builders" and He now has "become the chief cornerstone."[24] And to highlight the culpability of the Jewish leaders in this ignorance, while the verse in Ps 118.22 says that the stone was rejected by "the" builders, in Acts 4.11. Jesus is the stone rejected by "you (Gr = ὑμῶν) builders."

> [The Apostles] raised their voice to God with one accord and said, "Truly against Your holy Servant Jesus, whom You anointed, both Herod, and Pontius Pilate, and the Gentiles, and the people of Israel were gathered together to do whatever Your hand and Your purpose determined before to be done. (Acts 4.24–28)

In Acts 4.24–28, in a prayer to God, the Apostles acknowledge, to each other and to God that "Herod, and Pontius Pilate, and the Gentiles," and even "the people of Israel]" were gathered together to do whatever "Your hand and Your purpose determined before (Gr = προώρισεν; lit. = "predestined") to be done." All of the players, then, in the stories of the crucifixion were there doing what God had predetermined them to do. Chrysostom writes that the enemies of Christ "did not have power to do this, but you did it all."[25] He then goes on to write that "they gathered together as your enemies with murderous intent . . . but in fact they were doing what you wanted them to do."[26]

> And the high priest asked them, saying, "Did we not strictly command you not to teach in this name? And look, you have filled Jerusalem with your doctrine, and intend to bring this Man's blood on us." Then Peter and the *other* apostles answered and said: "We ought to obey God rather than men. The God of our fathers raised up Jesus whom you murdered by hanging on a tree. Him God has exalted to His right hand to *be* Prince and Savior to give repentance to Israel and forgiveness of sins. (Acts 5.27b–31)

There does not seem to be anything new here; just the continual conflict between the leaders of Israel and the Apostles—again told from the Apostles point of view. It seems that whatever the Apostles were teaching and preaching was being interpreted by the Jewish leaders as being accusatory to them concerning the crucifixion of Jesus. If this is an accurate portrayal of events, then the death of Jesus was not being perceived as the death of just another troublemaker but someone who some people recognized as someone who was telling the truth about who He was.

Perhaps the most interesting part of this text is the reply of the Apostles to the demand that they stop teaching about Jesus. They say that following His death on the cross, Jesus was exalted to God's right hand to be Prince and Savior for the purpose of giving "repentance to Israel and forgiveness of sin." For the religious leader's part, they undoubtedly believed that they had not committed a sin in putting Jesus to death and therefore had no need to repent. That being said, this text gives evidence that the Christian attitudes toward Jewish people's eligibility of God's grace had not yet hardened. At least here we hear the Apostles saying that Israel was not shut off from God's grace. This ambivalence would gradually disappear, and by the second and third centuries, most Christians were of the opinion that all Jewish people were culpable for the death of Jesus and abandoned by God in favor of the "new Israel."

> [Stephen said], "*You* stiff-necked and uncircumcised in heart and ears! You always resist the Holy Spirit; as your fathers *did*, so *do* you. Which of the prophets did your fathers not persecute? And they killed those who foretold the coming of the Just One, of whom you now have become the betrayers and murderers, who have received the law by the direction of angels and have not kept it." When they heard these things they were cut to the heart, and they gnashed at him with *their* teeth. . . . Then they cried out with a loud voice, stopped their ears, and ran at him with one accord; and cast *him* out of the city and stoned *him*. . . . Then [Stephen] cried out with a loud voice, "Lord, do not charge them with this sin." (Acts 7:51–54, 57–58a, 60)

As the animosity between Christians and the Jewish people continued to escalate, some within the Christian community saw the Jewish part in the crucifixion of Jesus as just the latest in a long history of violent resistance to God and God's messengers. This text can be seen as an early example of an indictment brought against all Jews for all time. In other words, from the beginning, the chosen people of God have resisted God's attempts to work with them—demonstrated by the way they treated the prophets sent to them in the past. The Christian author Arator, writing in the sixth century, commenting on this text wrote, "Insane, rebellious Judea, you hurl stones against Stephen, you who will always be stony because of your hard crime."[27] Other early Christian writers who turned their attention to what they considered the problems with the Jewish people, reasoned that since the earlier Jewish people continually turned their backs on God, and have now turned their back on God incarnate, then they certainly will continue to turn their backs on God in the future, leaving them with no hope for salvation.

However, here Stephen is only accusing earlier generations of Jewish people of turning their back on God. There is nothing here to suggest that future generations of Jewish people will continue to repeat the history of their ancestors. Still, what Stephen has said in this story is that Israel has never been the people God intended them to be and have always violently rejected God's messengers. He has, in effect, invalidated their religious and spiritual history. It is unrealistic to believe, then, that the religious leaders of first century Palestinian Judaism would hear this without a passionate, even visceral, response. To declare, with bellicosity, that your entire history is a lie is not something most people are prepared to hear, especially if it comes from a person you already suspect is trying to undermine your religion.

Therefore, if the Christians can (1) build a case against the Jewish people that they have always been recalcitrant to God and (2) construct a theology where God both punishes those who oppose Him and bless those who support Him, then the justification of later acts of violence against the Jews is not only correct and righteous but even meritorious. It has been proposed that later Christians used New Testament attacks on earlier generations of the Jewish people for this very justification.

> God anointed Jesus of Nazareth with the Holy Spirit and with power, who went about doing good and healing all who were oppressed by the devil, for God was with Him. And we are witnesses of all things which He did both in the land of the Jews and in Jerusalem, whom they killed by hanging on a tree. (Acts 10.38–39)

The author of the book of Acts here has Peter saying, in the hearing of the Roman centurion Cornelius and his men, that a Holy Spirit empowered Jesus was an innocent who despite, or perhaps because of his acts of goodness and healing, was put to death by the Jews. The crucifixion, then, is not only an act against God but a senseless act perpetrated by people who were unwilling to allow someone other than themselves to speak and act for God. Jesus was portrayed by the apostles as God's agent freeing people from their oppression from Satan. And in the midst of this good work, He was silenced. This, then, was a message not just for the new Christians but for the pagans as well. "This Lord that we are telling you about, who can and does heal loved ones, was put to death by the Jews." If there were any questions by the pagans as to who truly represented the true God, this story certainly would have tipped the scales in favor of the Christians. Not only was it specifically the Christians, but it was specifically not the Jews.

> Sons of the family of Abraham, and those . . . who fear God, to you the word of this salvation has been sent. For those who dwell in Jerusalem, and their rulers, because they did not know Him, nor even the voices of the Prophets which are read every Sabbath, have fulfilled *them* in condemning *Him*. And though they found no cause for death *in Him*, they asked Pilate that He should be put to death. (Acts 13.26–28)

Paul's account of what happened at the crucifixion of Jesus is perhaps the earliest Christian attempt at Christian *Heils-geschichte*. When he says that the Jewish leaders found "no cause for death" in Jesus but persuaded Pilate to crucify him anyway, he is, of course, writing from the newly developed Christians' belief that Jesus was sinless, and, therefore, not guilty of nor worthy of death. In the gospel accounts of the crucifixion, the Jewish leaders found Jesus guilty of blasphemy of the most onerous sort; claiming to be God, which, according to Jewish law, was punishable by death.

This evidence presents some troubling theological questions, and one of the questions might begin with this proposal: "If those held responsible for the crucifixion of Jesus were there at God's command and to fulfill His purpose, and if God is omniscient and knows the beginning from the end, then He would be aware of the millenniums of hatred, bigotry, forced migrations, pogroms, and holocaust inflicted upon the Jewish people, mostly as the hands of those who state that they are now the true people of God." Paul himself says that in condemning Jesus, the Jewish leaders were, perhaps unwittingly fulfilling God's plan both for Jesus and the entirety of God's creation. Paul's own reading of the Prophets of the Tanakh is that the condemnation of Jesus was foretold by the prophets, and his condemnation by the Jewish leaders was a fulfillment of these prophesies. It is more than interesting that the early Christian authors and later Christian authors can allow themselves to accuse the Jewish people of the crime of deicide while simultaneously also confessing that Jesus specifically came to die for the sins of humanity. It is this explicit divine predetermination of the death of Jesus that is heard repeatedly throughout the New Testament.

This, of course, raises questions about God's goodness, grace, forgiveness, and justice. I, as a Christian, do not have an answer to what is for me a theological conundrum—a theological conundrum, however, that is partially answered depending on how one views the question on the freedom or bondage of the will.

If one believes, as did Luther, that the human will is in bondage, then those who perpetrated the acts of evil against the Jewish people were doing what their basest, and some would say natural, inclinations led them to do. This does not excuse them but does explain, partially, why they continued to inflict the damage on the Jewish people over the centuries.

Of course, for the growing number of Christians who believe that the Creation/Fall story, as recorded in Genesis, is a myth, the explanation(s) of Christian anti-Semitism may not even have anything to do with a free or fallen human nature but is part of the long story of humanity that is both shameful and lamentable.

Yet modern Christians who believe that anti-Semitism is wrong and evil continue to witness Christians demonstrating in a number of ways that they still are haters of the Jewish people. Very few Christians would be willing to conclude that the grace of God is not able to overcome this evil. They, therefore, are left to believe that these "Christians" are experiencing or are being taught a Christianity that is aberrant, for it does not reflect the grace of God as they understand it.

That, then, brings us to those modern "Christians," who see nothing wrong with "civilized" acts of anti-Semitism and are unsympathetic to the plight with which many Jewish people have lived and do live. This author, as a Christian, is reluctant but must admit that the number of these "Christians" is not altogether small.

The Charge of Deicide in the Epistles

A reading of the Pauline epistles reveals only one text where Paul is unequivocal about the Jewish people's responsibility in the death of Jesus.

> For you, brethren, became imitators of the churches of God which are in Judea in Christ Jesus. For you also suffered the same things from your own countrymen, just as they did from the Jews, who killed both the Lord and their own prophets, and have persecuted us; and they do not please God and are contrary to all men, forbidding us to speak to the Gentiles that they may be saved, so as always to fill up *the measure of* their sins, but wrath has come upon them to the uttermost. (1 Thess: 2.14–16)

Paul, in this passage, wants the believers in Thessalonica to know that they are not alone in the persecution and abuse they are suffering for their faith. He too, from his "own countrymen," has faced conflict over his desire to share the gospel with the Gentile population in Jerusalem and Judea. However, in this passage, Paul seems to forget temporarily that he is speaking to suffering believers and unburdens himself of the anger he feels towards the Jewish people in Judea, who are guilty, in one highly charged condemnatory swoop, of (1) killing Jesus Christ, (2) killing earlier prophets sent from God, (3) persecuting those who are presently carrying the gospel to the Gentiles, (4) not pleasing God, (5) being contrary to all men, (6) attempting to halt the spread of the gospel, and (7) "filling up the measure of their sins." All of this in one short sentence! Because of these sins, then, wrath has come upon them (assumingly from God) "to the uttermost." The Greek of this final phrase raises some very important questions as to what Paul was actually saying about the wrath that he believes the Jewish people are experiencing. The Greek phrase that Paul uses is ἔφθασεν δὲ ἐπ' αὐτοὺς ἡ ὀργὴ εἰς τέλος, which literally translates to "but the wrath came on them to the end."

For those tempted to interpret Paul's words to mean that the Jewish people will suffer for these sins to the end of the age—code for "the end of time" (which in the Greek is συντέλεια αἰῶνός)—the verb φθάνω is in the first aorist tense, so it literally means that the wrath has already come and is complete. The argument against a future, never-ending wrath upon the Jews is strengthened if Thayer is correct by suggesting that the noun τέλος means "always of the end of some act or state, *but not of the end of a period of time*"[28] (emphasis added). Thayer also writes that when εἰς τέλος is used in Scripture, it means "to the very end appointed for these evils," and in 1 Thess 2.16 it means "to the (procurement of their) end, that is to destruction."[29]

Therefore, if the wrath has already come upon the Jewish people, and if they have brought this destruction upon themselves, it is possible to interpret Paul's words to mean that the Jewish people present at the crucifixion hold some responsibility in the death of Jesus. Their participation in the crucifixion has separated them from God, and that separation is itself the wrath that has come. However, that interpretation would require that the interpreter ignore what Paul has to say in later epistles about the love, forgiveness, grace, and blood of Jesus being shed for all of humanity, "for the Jew first, and then for the Greek."[30] Further, if, as many commentators believe, that Paul wrote 1 Thess in C.E. 51, then the wrath is not the destruction of Jerusalem and the Temple, which were destroyed in C.E. 70.[31] Setzer believes that in this text Paul is saying that it is "Israel's [continual] persecution of the righteous and prophets" that is responsible for "filling up the measure of Israel's sins and Israel's present affliction [is] punishment for her guilt."[32] The most obvious affliction in C.E. 51 is the continual occupation of Israel by the Roman Empire, not the destruction of Jerusalem and the Temple.

However, using what seems to be a fairly accepted hermeneutic principle that a theological position not be based on a single text, Hagner goes on to explore Paul's understanding of Israel, based on their history, and their continued place in God's *heils geschichte*. Hagner concludes that "Anti-Judaism is part and parcel of Paul's theological position."[33] Yet this break with Judaism "must in no sense be taken to mean that Paul had turned against his people or against his Jewish heritage," and "if this is true, it is all the more inappropriate to connect Paul with anti-Semitism of any kind."[34]

Divine Predetermination in the Epistles

The ability of first to twenty-first century Christians to continue to hold onto the belief that the Jewish people acted immorally in the death of Jesus, while simultaneously believing that the death of Jesus was preordained by God, opens up a number of questions the answers to which may prove to be unsettling. For example,

Is the insistence of blaming the Jewish people for the murder of Jesus an attempt to exonerate God from a divine responsibility for the death of God? Consider the following texts.

God set [Jesus] forth to be a propitiation (ἱλαστήριον; lit. = "relating to appeasing or expiating, having placating or expiating force, expiatory"[35]) by His blood, through faith, to demonstrate His righteousness, because of His forbearance previously committed. (Rom 3.25)

[Jesus] was delivered up because of our offenses, and was raised because of our justification. (Rom 4.25)

But God demonstrates His own love toward us, in that while we were still sinners, Christ died for us. Much more then, having now been justified by His blood, we shall be saved from wrath through Him. For if when we were enemies we were reconciled too God through the death of His Son, much more, having been reconciled, we shall be saved by His live. (Rom 5.8–10)

For what the law could not do in that it was weak through the flesh, God did by sending His own Son in the likeness of sinful flesh, on account of sin: He condemned sin in the flesh. (Rom 8.3)

He who did not spare His own Son, but delivered Him up for us all, how shall He not with Him also freely give us all things? (Rom 8.32)

For [God] made [Christ] who knew no sin to be sin for us, that we might become the righteousness of God in Him. (2 Cor 5.21)

Grace to you and peace from God the Father of our Lord Jesus Christ, who gave Himself for our sins, that He might deliver us from this present evil age, according to the will of our God and Father. (Gal 1.3–4)

But when the fullness of the time had come, God sent forth His Son, born of a woman, born under the law, to redeem those who were under the law, that we might receive the adoption as sons. (Gal 4.4–5)

For it pleased the Father that in Him all the fullness should dwell, and by Him to reconcile all things to Himself, by Him, whether things on earth or things in heaven, having made peace through the blood of His cross. And you, who were once alienated and enemies in your mind by wicked works, yet now He has reconciled in the body of His flesh through death, to present you holy, and blameless, and irreproachable in His sight. (Col 1.19–22)

In each of these texts it is God, in council with Jesus, who determined that it was only through the blood of Jesus that humanity could be saved. There does not seem to be another alternative plan. Jesus must die for atonement for sins to happen. Further, if Paul can be considered one of the most important apostles and one of the earliest articulators of Christian soteriology, then when he says nine times, to three different churches, that this was God's plan, we can assume that other Christians listened.

Paul was not alone in his belief that the primary purpose of the incarnation was to secure salvation for the entire world through the death of Jesus. This is heard in the non-Pauline epistles as well.

> Of this salvation the prophets have inquired and searched diligently, who prophesied of the grace that would come to you, searching what, or what manner of time, indicating when He testified beforehand the sufferings of Christ and the glories that would follow. (1 Pet 1.10–11)

> [Christ] indeed was foreordained before the foundation of the world, but was manifest in these last times for you who through Him believe in God, who raised Him from the dead and gave Him glory, so that your faith and hope are in God. (1 Pet 1.17–21)

> And [Christ] Himself is the propitiation for our sins, and not for ours only but also for the whole world. (1 Jhn 2.1–2)

> Not with the blood of goats and calves, but with His own blood He entered the Most Holy Place once for all, having obtained eternal redemption. For if the blood of bulls and goats and the ashes of a heifer, sprinkling the unclean, sanctifies for the purifying of the flesh, how much more shall the blood of Christ, who through the eternal Spirit offered Himself without spot to God? (Heb 9.12–14)

Therefore, not only was the death of Jesus done with the full knowledge of God, but with God's blessings, and billions of Christians who have lived from the first century to today have interpreted the sending of the divine Son to this earth to die for our sins as an act of unspeakable and matchless love on the part of God.

Therefore, those Christians who believe that the Bible is the divine word of God are left with that word saying that both God and the Jewish people are responsible for the death of Jesus. Yet in the New Testament; in the Gospels, in the Book of Acts, and in the Epistles, when the crucifixion is mentioned, God is praised and/or the Jews are blamed.

It is possible that both early and modern Christians have not fully, intellectually, and emotionally rectified what the New Testament writers have to say about the crucifixion of God. The overwhelming majority of Christians have believed and do believe that the death of Jesus was not just the death of a good and righteous man. Their reading of the New Testament has led them to believe that the death of Jesus was necessary for their salvation, and in that sense, it was a good thing. Yet the New Testament tells a story of the death of Jesus that is not peaceful or serene. He did not wish a farewell to his disciples and walk into the desert and disappear from history. Instead we are given a story of him being repeatedly brutalized, beaten, mocked, and subjected to a most horrible death, and in the years, weeks, days, and hours leading up to this climactic event, the readers of the New Testament are told that the Jewish leaders hounded, threatened, and charged Jesus with all manner of crimes. They sought to trap him in his words and charged him with blasphemy. They are the ones who brought him before Pilate and Herod. They are portrayed as the ones who followed Jesus to Golgotha and continually screamed at and mocked him. Therefore, although the death of Jesus is a good thing, the manner of his death, as portrayed in the Gospels, is not a dispassionate story. The authors of the New Testament are almost bewildered by the reactions of the Jewish people toward Jesus, even though Jesus told stories of his betrayal. They say, in various ways, that Israel was in a privileged position. They were the chosen people of God, and because they were the chosen people of God, they should have accepted Jesus and worshiped him. Yet as told in the New Testament, not only did they not accept him, but they scorned and crucified him. So it is perhaps this final act of betrayal against God, and God's Son, that causes the writers of the Book of Acts and the epistles to spend time blaming the Jews for the death of Jesus, and charging them with deicide. But in doing so, they have either forgotten or neglected to consider that Jesus foretold them repeatedly that his betrayal and death was a fulfillment of prophesy.[36] Would God condemn his own chosen, covenant people for fulfilling divinely inspired prophesies told hundreds of years earlier?[37] One has to conclude that although the post-crucifix followers of God charge the Jewish people with deicide, God does not. This charge, then, of deicide leveled at the Jewish people, is an evil that does not carry a divine sanction, and must, therefore, be eradicated from Christian language, liturgy, hymnology, and theology.

Hope for Israel's Salvation

The Book of Acts

Twice, after his crucifixion and before his ascension, Jesus commands his disciples to take his story to others to make them disciples as well. In Mt 28.19 he says, "Go therefore and make disciples of all the nations, baptizing them in the name of the Father and of the Son and of the Holy Spirit." In Acts 1.8 Jesus says to the disciples, "And you shall be witnesses to Me in Jerusalem, and in all Judea, and Samaria, and to the end of the earth." What is significant about these verses is the insistence of Jesus that his gospel (witness) be taken not only to the non-Jewish population but to the Jewish population as well. In both of these texts, the Jewish people are not excluded, and in the Acts text, they are specifically included as recipients of this message. The obvious conclusion, then, is that if Jesus viewed the Jewish people as hopelessly lost and irredeemable, he would not have bothered to send his disciples to preach to them. He was still interested in them as a people and interested in their salvation.

The repetition of the inclusion of Israel as recipients of the gospel message in the book of Acts represents a belief that the Jewish people were, now along with the Gentiles, a significant part of God's kingdom. However, the Jewish people needed to understand, according to the early disciples, that continued inclusion in God's kingdom was faith in Jesus Christ.

The texts that speak of the continued hope for Israel follows:

> Therefore, when [the apostles] had come together, they asked [Jesus], saying, "Lord, will You at this time restore the kingdom to Israel?" And He said to them, "It is not for you to know times or seasons which the Father has put in His own authority. But you shall receive power when the Holy Spirit has come upon you; and you shall be witnesses to Me in Jerusalem, and in all Judea and Samaria, and to the end of the earth." (Acts 1.6–8)

Both the question of the apostles and the response of Jesus deserve attention here. This question about the restoration of Israel is asked with the expectation that Israel will at sometime in the future will be restored by Jesus. Israel has not passed beyond the pale of acceptance by God, and the apostles are expecting Jesus to restore Israel. If they believed that Israel was no longer of interest to God, they would not have asked the question. Further, this question is asked by these men before Paul had created the language of Christians being the "new Israel."

Although Jesus does not directly answer the question of the apostles, he tells them that, empowered by the Spirit, they will witness to Jesus in "Jerusalem, Judea and Samaria, and to the end of the earth." While no one will suggest that non-Jews did not live in Jerusalem or Judea, it would be difficult to conclude that only the non-Jews were to receive the witness of the apostles. Indeed, in Acts 1–9 the primary audience of the preaching of the apostles is the Jewish people. This is a fairly clear sign that both God and the apostles were interested in witnessing to the Jewish people about Jesus. Even Paul, who because of continued resistance to the gospel threatened to no longer bother with them, repeatedly witnessed to the Jewish people in their synagogues. Yet even if he had stopped, that does not mean that all witness to the Jewish people stopped. As a matter of fact, Peter, who was given the responsibility of witnessing to the Jewish people, never had that call rescinded.

All of this evidence, then, suggests that the declaration that will be heard from many of the early Church Fathers that the gospel was never intended for the Jews is simply wrong.

> Men of Israel, hear these words. . . . Repent, and let every one of you be baptized in the name of Jesus Christ for the remission of sins, and you shall receive the gift of the Holy Spirit. For the promise is to you and to your children, and to all who are afar off, as many as the Lord our God will call. (Acts 2.22, 38-39)

The call to the "men of Israel" to repent and be baptized is further evidence that the Jewish people were, along with those "who are afar off," not irredeemable. However, Peter's declaration that the promise of God is not just to the men of Israel, but to their children as well, is perhaps one of the most important statements in the New Testament about the future relations between the Jewish people and the Christians. Even though Peter is saying that the promise continues for future generations of Jewish people only if they accept Jesus Christ, that is also true for all peoples, including those who "are afar off." Therefore, Jewish people in the second, fifth, eighth, thirteenth, twentieth, and twenty-first century can still be recipients of the promise.³⁸ Therefore, according to the Apostle to the Gentiles and the Apostle to the Jews, there will never be a time when the Jewish people are no longer eligible to receive the promise of God.

> Yet now, brethren, I know that you [crucified Jesus] in ignorance as did also your rulers.³⁹ But those things which God foretold by the mouth of all His prophets, that the Christ would suffer, He has thus fulfilled. Repent therefore and be converted, that your sins may be blotted out (Gr = ἐξαλειφθῆναι; lit = to be removed) so that times of refreshing may come from the presence of the Lord. (Acts 3.17–21)

This call for repentance and conversion is followed by the promise that that act of repentance will cause God to blot out their sins. The images that might very likely have presented themselves to a first century Jewish person, when he/she heard of sins being removed following an act of repentance, were the ones involved in the Day of Atonement, where sin was symbolically removed from the camp and the people (see Lev 16) and transferred to the head of the scapegoat. Interpreting the symbolic acts of that day the author(s) of Lev 16.30–31 says, "For on that day the priest shall make atonement for you to cleanse you that you may be clean from all your sins before the Lord. It is a Sabbath of solemn rest for you, and you shall afflict your souls. It is a statue forever." Peter, then, is saying to the assembled people that that forgiveness and cleansing from *all* sins can still be had, and that the gift of the Holy Spirit will follow and bring a refreshing from God. This is not the language one give to a people who were considered eternally damned by God, and removed from God's presence.

Also, in this text, Peter says that the people who were responsible for the crucifixion carried out this act out of ignorance (Gr = κατά ἄγνοιαν ἐπράξατε; lit = you acted according to ignorance). If Peter is correct that those responsible for the crucifixion were unaware of what they were doing, that is, killing God (deicide), then the intimation of the Gospels of the premeditation of the murder of Jesus needs to be reexamined. Ambrosiaster writes that the Jews "did not accept Christ because they were mistaken, not because there was any malice on their part."⁴⁰ What can be concluded from this declaration by Peter is that what the leaders understood themselves to be doing was silencing a dangerous rebel who was intent on destabilizing the peace the leaders had reached with the Roman authorities. For them, handing Jesus over to be crucified was an act of national survival, not an act of deicide.

> You [people of Israel] are sons of the prophets and of the covenant which God made with our fathers, saying to Abraham, "And in your seed all the families of the earth shall be blessed." To your first, God, having raised up His Servant Jesus, sent Him to bless you, in turning sway everyone of you from your iniquities. (Acts 3.25–26)

As Peter continues his speech, he reminds his hearers of their privileged position with God in the past. They are the children of Abraham, the father of the people called by God, and therefore, members the covenant. Therefore, just as God spoke to Abraham, so God continued to speak to his people through the prophets. All first century Jewish people were the inheritors of those traditions, but their blessedness with God continues, says Peter, if they now turn to Christ, for they are the people God first sent Jesus to, to bless and turn away from their wickedness.

In this text, Peter also recounts all the guilty parties who he believes had "gathered together" against Jesus, and in this list, the "people of Israel" are listed last, preceded by "Herod, and Pontius Pilate, with the Gentiles." Therefore, if, for the Christians, those responsible for the death of Jesus Christ, are guilty of deicide, then the Gentiles, those now grafted into the house of Israel, are also guilty of the same crime. This, of course, resonates with the theological tradition that it was the sins of all of humanity that sent Jesus Christ to the cross.[41]

This same message, that the gospel was specifically sent first to Israel, is repeated in Acts 5.31, where Peter tells the people that God raised up Jesus to "give repentance to Israel and forgiveness of sins." In Acts 10, Peter says that the message of peace through Jesus Christ, "which was proclaimed throughout all Judea" was "sent to the children of Israel." Acts 11.19 is of particular interest, for there it says that "those who were scattered after the persecution that arose over Stephen traveled as far as Phoenicia, Cyprus, and Antioch, *preaching the word to no one but the Jews only*" (emphasis added).

Finally Paul, in the synagogue in Antioch in Pisidia, in Acts 13.26, says to the worshipers, "To you the word of this salvation has been sent." He continues in vv.32–33a by saying, "And we declare to you glad tidings—that promise which was made to the fathers. God has fulfilled this for us their children, in that He has raised up Jesus." Hare, in discussing Paul's attitude toward the Jewish people says that Paul's early optimism "was *theologically grounded* in the intensely held conviction that the God whose eschatological messenger had been refused by Israel, had nonetheless *not* abandoned his people" (emphasis in original).[42]

The Pauline Epistles

The Apostle Paul is intent on repeating, in his epistles, that the sacrifice of Jesus on the cross was, in fact, the sacrifice of God, and that sacrifice has brought both the Jews and Greeks under God. Now, both the Jews and Greeks stand both condemned and blessed under God. When the Apostle Paul writes about deliverance for the Jewish people, it is predominantly in the context of the full, cosmic efficaciousness of the atonement of Christ for all of humanity. Salvation is now, through Christ, available to both the Jew and the Greek. Abraham, for Paul, is now the *spiritual* father of all who believe in Christ, and Abraham, the spiritual father, supersedes Abraham, the purely Jewish father. Paul's articulation of this is seen in the following texts.

For I am not ashamed of the gospel of Christ, for it is the power of God to salvation for everyone who believes, for the Jew first and also for the Greek. (Rom 1.16)

Tribulation and anguish, on every soul of man who does evil, of the Jew first and also of the Greek; but glory, honor, and peace to everyone who works good, to the Jew first and also to the Greek. (Rom 2.9)

What then? Are we better than [the Jews]? Not at all. For we have previously charged both Jews and Greeks that they are all under sin. (Rom 3.9)

Or is He the God of the Jews only? Is He not also the God of the Gentiles? Yes, of the Gentiles, also, since there is one God who will justify the circumcised and the uncircumcised through faith. (Rom 3.29, 30)

Therefore it is of faith that it might be according to grace, so that the promise might be sure to all the seed, not only to those who are of the law, but also to those who are of the faith of Abraham, who is the father of us all. (Rom 4.16)

What if God, wanting to show His wrath and to make His power known, endured with much longsuffering the vessels of wrath prepared for suffering, and that He might make known the riches of His glory on the vessels of mercy, which He had prepared beforehand for glory, even us whom He called, not of the Jews only, but also of the Gentiles? (Rom 9.22–24)

Brethren, my hearts desire and prayer to God for Israel is that they may be saved. For I bear them witness that they have a zeal for God, but not according to knowledge. For they being ignorant of God's righteousness, in seeking to establish their own righteousness, have not submitted to the righteousness of God. For Christ is the end of the law for righteousness to everyone who believes. (Rom 10.1–4)

For there is not distinction between Jew and Greek, for the same Lord over all is rich to all who call upon Him. For "whoever calls upon the name of the Lord will be saved." (Rom 10.12-13)

I say then, has God cast way His people? Certainly not! For I also am an Israelite, of the seed of Abraham, of the tribe of Benjamin. God has not cast away His people whom He foreknew. . . . Even so then, at this present time there is a remnant according to the election of grace. . . . I say then, have they stumbled that they should fall? Certainly not! But through their fall, to provoke them to jealousy, salvation has come to the Gentiles. Now if their fall is riches for the work, and their failure riches for the Gentiles, how much more their fullness! For I speak to you Gentiles; inasmuch as I am an apostle to the Gentiles, I magnify my ministry, if by any means I may provoke to jealousy those who are my flesh and save some of them. For if their being cast away is the reconciling of the word, what will their acceptance be but life from the dead? For if the first fruit is holy, the lump is also holy: and if the root is holy, so are the branches. And if some of the branches were broken off, and you, being a wild olive tree, were grafted in among them, and with them became a partaker of the root and fatness of the olive tree, do not boast against the branches. But if you boast, remember that you do not support the root, but the root supports you. You will say then, "Branches were broken off that I might be grafted in." Well said. Because of unbelief they were broken off, and you stand by faith. Do not be haughty, but fear. For if God did not spare the natural branches, He may not spare you either. Therefore consider the goodness and severity of God: on those who fell, severity; but toward you, goodness, if you continue in His goodness. Otherwise, you also will be cut off. And they also, if they do not continue in unbelief, will be grafted in, for God is able to graft them in again. For if you were cut out of the olive tree which is wild by nature, and were grafted contrary to nature into a good olive tree, how much more will these, who are the natural branches, be grafted into their own olive tree? For I do not desire, brethren, that you should be ignorant of this mystery, lest you should be wise in your own option, that hardening in part has happened to Israel until the fullness of the Gentiles has come in. And so all Israel will be saved, as it is written: "The Deliverer will come out of Zion, and he will turn away ungodliness from Jacob; For this is My covenant with them, When I take away their sins." Concerning the gospel they are enemies for you sake, but concerning the election they are beloved for the sake of their fathers. For the gifts and the calling for God are irrevocable. For as you were once disobedient to God, yet have now obtained mercy through their disobedience, even so these also have now been disobedient, that through the mercy shown you they also may obtain mercy. For God has commuted them all to disobedience, that He might have mercy on all. (Rom 11.1–32)

For He who worked effectively in Peter for the apostleship to the circumcised also worked effectively in me towards the Gentiles. (Gal 2.8)

For you are all sons of God through faith in Christ Jesus. For as many of you as were baptized into Christ have put on Christ. There is neither Jew nor Greek, there is neither slave nor free, there is neither male nor female; for you are all one in Christ Jesus. (Gal 3.26–28)

For He Himself is our peace, who has made both one, and has broken down the middle wall of division between us, having abolished in His flesh the enmity . . . so as to create in Himself one new man from the two, thus making peace, and that He might reconcile them both to God in one body through the cross. . . . And He came and preached peace to you who were afar off and to those who were near. For through Him we both have access through one Spirit to the Father. Now, therefore, you are no longer strangers and foreigners but fellow citizens with the saints and members of the household of God. (Eph 2.14–19)

[God] made known to me the mystery . . . that the Gentiles would be fellow heirs of the same body, and partakers of His promise in Christ through the gospel. (Eph 3.3, 6)

You have put off the old man . . . and have put on the new man . . . where there is neither Greek nor Jew, circumcised nor uncircumcised, barbarian, Scythian, slave nor free, but Christ is all and in all. (Col 3.9–11)

At least two elements of Paul's *heils-geschicte* are revealed in these texts, *viz.*, Israel has been and continues to be God's chosen people, and the Abrahamic covenant has not been cancelled.

There are Church Fathers who are able to agree with Paul. In his commentary on Rom 11.1 Ambrosiaster writes:

> Since Paul has shown that the people of Israel did not believe, now, in order that it should not be thought that he has said that they were all unbelievers, he shows that God has not rejected the inheritance which he promised to the descendents of Abraham. For he would not have promised them a kingdom if he knew that none of them would believe. . . . By using himself as an example, he shows that the part of Israel which God foreknew would be saved had in fact been saved and that the part which had been consigned to perdition because of its constant unbelief might yet be saved.[43]

Theodoret of Cyr, insisting on the continual viability of Israel's covenant with God, reads Paul as saying that "if God had rejected his people, he would he (Paul) would have been one of the rejected as well."[44] He goes on to say, "Paul could have supported his statement by referring to the 3,000 who believed at Jerusalem and to the many thousands spoken of by St. James, not to mention all those Jews of the Diaspora who believed the message."[45] Even Chrysostom, who preached eight homilies against the Jews, writes, "For nobody will deny that they have sinned greatly. But let us see if the fall is of such a kind as to be incurable. . . . No, it is not!"[46] And Pelagius says, "They (Israel) have not fallen away completely and beyond hope."[47]

Origen, Eusebius of Caesarea, and Augustine are but three who understand Paul to be saying that in the post-crucifix *heils-geschicte* Jews and Gentiles all stand before God—equally condemned and equally eligible for salvation. Origen writes, "Not only the Gentiles are benefited by the coming of Christ but also some who belong to the divine race, many of whom have been called to salvation."[48] He says in another place, "For the Israelites, although they rejected their redeemer and stoned and persecuted those who were sent to them, nevertheless still contain a remnant within them."[49] Eusebius agrees and says, "The remnant of the Jews has proclaimed the sign of the Lord to all the Gentiles and has joined to God in one people, drawn to him."[50] This language of the remnant is also heard in Augustine, where he says, "The remnant refers to the Jews who have believed in Christ. Many of them did believe in the days of the apostles, and even today there are some converts, though very few."[51] However, Theodoret of Cyr argues that the remnant does not mean "very few" but says, "So it is not unbelievable that you too are ignorant of how many Jews have believed in the Saviour."[52] Pelagius comes to the same conclusion and says that "Israel *as a whole* has not obtained righteousness"[53] (emphasis added). And finally, Diodore writes, "Only a remnant obtained the grace of the promise."[54]

Even though it is difficult to reconcile some of the statements of the apostle in Rom 11, the gist of his argument in all of these texts is that both Jews and Greeks now stand together before God, with neither having a spiritual advantage. All will be condemned through disobedience, and all will be blessed through grace. This is the second element of his salvation history. The Early Fathers who agree include Ambrosiaster who writes that "although Paul puts the Jews first because of their ancestors, nevertheless he says that they must also accept the gift of the gospel in the same way as the Gentiles."[55] He goes on to say that for Paul, "In general everyone is lumped together because of unbelief or else exalted together because of their belief."[56] Pelagius, commenting on Rom 3.9, writes, "Both Jews and Gentiles are under sin—something we not only deduce by reason but also corroborate by the witness of the Jews themselves."[57] In an earlier commentary Origen writes, "Not only does Paul say that there is only one God for both Jews and Gentiles, but he adds that this God is the one who justifies the circumcised on the ground of their faith and the uncircumcised through their faith."[58]

It is apparent that the canonical writers spent time thinking about these things, and it is reasonable to believe that these issues came up in discussions. The conversations among the Christians in Acts 15 are evidence of this. What is most compelling is the ability of the early Christians to juxtapose (successfully?) the charges of deicide and divine predetermination. In other words, the Jewish people, in these New Testament texts, are repeatedly charged with killing the God of the Christians; Jesus Christ. Yet, they are equally adamant that the principle reason for the incarnation was for God to die for God's people—both Jews and non-Jews. While various soteriologies developed over the first few centuries, those found in the New Testament, principally in the writings of the apostle Paul, unequivocally declare that Jesus came to die for our sins. This was the divine plan; this was the divine predetermination—the divine predetermination—that would have been somehow thwarted had Jesus not died.

Finally, standing next to these two themes is a third one that is also somewhat curious. Again, principally in Paul's letters to the Romans, Galatians, Ephesians, and Colossians, continued hope for Israel's salvation through Jesus Christ appears.

In one sentence, it may be summed up in this manner. Even though God and Jesus Christ predetermined that salvation for all of humanity could only happen through the sacrificial life and death of Jesus, the principle architects of the actual crucifixion, the Jewish leaders, were more than just willing instruments in the hands of God. They were savage and mad in their lust for the blood of Jesus. Yet, even though the Jews crucified God, they still may be recipients of God's grace.

Conclusion

The theological disciples of the Apostle Paul have grown the enormity of the crucifixion to a degree that has allowed later Christians to globalize this event geographically, chronologically, and spiritually to say that all Jews for all times are guilty of the death of Jesus, the self-proclaimed "I AM" (ἐγὼ εἰμί), and are therefore guilty of deicide. This globalization is not heard either in the gospels, the Acts or the epistles, but in later Christian authors. The New Testament writers seemed content to lay the blame either on the Jewish leaders who actually took part of the crucifixion or, at the most, contemporary, first century Jews. It seems that to widen a net of blame from a few men in Palestine in the first century to the millions of Jewish people who have suffered, and who continue to suffer at the hands of Christians speaks of both a theology (Who is God?) and an anthropology and psychology (Who are humans?) that needs to be explored. In other words, is there, within the human psyche an archetypical racism that is given reign at the slightest provocation, and when questions of God and salvation become part of the matrix, it erupts into acts of brutality that denies everything the Bible tells us about who God is? Is the continual hatred of Christians directed toward the Jewish religion only theological or is it also racial? Does racism trump all other beliefs, and can that hatred be justified by a reading of the New Testament text?

If I have learned one thing in my years of teaching classes in early Christianity, it is that hermeneutic can be created that allows the creators of those hermeneutic to justify almost any act, because it is also, according to that hermeneutic, justified by sacred Scripture or God or both. This is true not only of Christians but of all believers who have a sacred Scripture as an integral part of their belief system. All believers, who bother to read their sacred Scriptures, begin with presuppositions, which inform their hermeneutic, which is used to do exegesis, and part of my hermeneutic in working through this part of this book is that there is no justification for the continual hatred and suspicion directed toward the Jewish religion or people that can be justified by the word of God.

In the early centuries of Christianity, many writers taught that women were guilty of seducing men simply because they existed. In the antebellum South, Black people were guilty of immoral and/or criminal behavior, simply because they existed. Many Christians have embraced this same belief against the Jewish people; they are guilty before God simply because they exist.

However, I believe that there is a way to interpret the New Testament that allows both Christians and Jews to continue to hold onto their sacred beliefs and do so in ways that do not carry inherent vitriol towards each other.

Notes

1. Marvin Perry and Frederick M. Schweitzer, *Antisemitism: Myth and Hate from Antiquity to the Present* (New York: Palgrave MacMillan, 2002), 18.

2. John Dominic Crossan, *Who Killed Jesus? Exposing the Roots of Anti-Semitism in the Gospel Story of the Death of Jesus* (San Francisco, CA: HarperSanFrancisco, 1995).

3. The Gnostics are the most notable example of early Christians who either espoused what came to be considered unorthodox christologies, or who, for theological reasons could not allow their Savior to have a σῶμα (carnal body).

4. It is difficult to believe that the Jewish people were the first people to be charged with deicide. Some fifth century Athenians may have been considered Socrates to be guilty of the same crime. However, in a monotheistic religion, a charge of deicide carries with it far more serious consequences.

5. It is far more likely that first century Jewish people living in the Diaspora, and especially in the Greek speaking Diaspora, would have an appreciation for the value of the writings of the Greek philosophers, both ancient and contemporary. Many, if not most, of the early church Fathers praise the writings of either Plato or Aristotle or the Stoics. However, one would be hard pressed to find evidence that they allowed the writings of the philosophers be on a theological par with what they considered the word of God.

6. Ἀπόστολος = "a delegate, messenger, one sent forth with orders." Thayer writes that this word "specially applied to the twelve disciples whom Christ selected . . . to be his constant companions and heralds to proclaim to men the kingdom of God." J. H. Thayer, *A Greek-English Lexicon of the New Testament* (Grand Rapids, MI: Zondervan Publishing House, 1885), 68.

7. In the Nag Hammadi Library alone there is the Gospel of Truth, the Gospel of Thomas, The Gospel of Philip, the Gospel of the Egyptians, and the Gospel of Mary.

8. Many early Christian authors begin to quote texts from other, earlier Christian texts in a way that suggests they view them as authoritative. Both Catholic and non-Catholic authors and documents vary as to which books are acceptable. What follows is a partial list of authors and documents that either mention or quote texts as authoritative. Chronologically they are: Ignatius of Antioch (early 2nd c.), Polycarp (early 2nd c.), Marcion (mid 2nd c.), Valentinus (mid 2nd c.), Justin Martyr (mid 2nd c.), Irenaeus (late 2nd c.), Clement of Alexandria (late 2nd c.), Tertullian (early 3rd c.), Muratorian Canon (3rd c.), Origen (late 3rd–early 4th c.), Eusebius (early 4th c.), Codex Sinaiticus (mid 4th c.), Athanasius (late 4th c.), Didymus the Blind (late 4th c.), Peshitta (early 5th c.), and the Vulgate (early 5th c.).

9. Tertullian, in the second century wrote, "From this, therefore, do we draw up our rule. Since the Lord Jesus Christ sent the apostles to preach, (our rule is) that no others ought to be received as preachers than those whom Christ appointed; for 'no man knoweth the Father save the Son, and he to whomsoever the Son will reveal Him.' Nor does the Son seem to have revealed Him to any other than the apostles, whom He sent forth to preach—that, of course, which He revealed to them. Now, what that was which they preached—in other words, what it was which Christ revealed to them—can, as I must here likewise prescribe, properly be proved in no other way than by those very churches which the apostles rounded in person, by declaring the gospel to them directly themselves, both viva voce [living voice], as the phrase is, and subsequently by their epistles. If, then, these things are so, it is in the same degree manifest that all doctrine which agrees with the apostolic churches-those moulds and original sources of the faith must be reckoned for truth, as undoubtedly containing that which the (said) churches received from the apostles, the apostles from Christ, Christ from God. Whereas all doctrine must be prejudged as false which saviors of contrariety to the truth of the churches and apostles of Christ and God. It remains, then, that we demonstrate whether this doctrine of ours, of which we have now given the rule, has its origin in the tradition of the apostles, and whether all other *doctrines* do not *ipso facto* proceed from falsehood. We hold communion with the apostolic churches because our doctrine is in no respect different *from theirs*. This is our witness of truth." Tertullian, *The Prescription against the Heretics*, Ch. 21.

10. The author of the first century "Epistle to the Ephesians" refers to the apostles as "holy apostles" (Eph 3.15).

11. The author of the "Second Epistle of Peter" speaks of Paul's writings as scriptural (2 Pet 3.16).

12. This would, of course, not be true of the Gnostic Christians, who believed that all flesh was carnal, and a creation of an evil demigod. For these Gnostic Christians the purpose for the coming of Jesus was to reveal the Father, not to die on a cross.

13. Leon Sheleff writes, "There might well have been anti-Semitism without the crucifixion, given that the Jews were almost the prototype of a minority group. . . . But the cross was the ever-present symbol, the constant reminder not just of Jesus' death but of those who were assumed to bear responsibility for the deed." Leon Sheleff, *In the Shadow of the Cross: Jewish-Christian Relations Through the Ages* (London: Vallentine Mitchell, 2004), 11.

14. Weddig Fricke, *The Court Martial of Jesus: A Christian Defends the Jews Against the Charge of Deicide* (New York: Grove Weidenfeld, 1987), 222.

15. Sheleff, *In the Shadows of the Cross*, 11. The recent increased, scholarly attention being given to the Gospel of Judas has added another voice to this debate. See: Elaine Pagels and Karen L. King, *Reading Judas: The Gospel of Judas and the Shaping of Christianity* (New York: Viking Press, 2007).

16. Although the "multitude" is never specifically identified as Jewish, it can be assumed that during one of the holy days on the Jewish calendar, the multitude was predominantly Jewish rather than gentile.

17. Ibid., 35. In his chapter "Crucifixion," Sheleff looks at literary, theological, and canonical questions to demonstrate the difficulty of placing blame for the crucifixion on the Jews and concludes that that the crucifixion found in the canonical gospels may be an example of revisionist history. See pp. 35–64.

18. Although the question is far from settled, many scholars now believe that Luke is the author of Acts. The lack of the mention of the outcome of the trial of Paul in Rome (C.E. 62), the persecution under the Emperor Nero (C.E. 64), Paul's death (C.E. 68), or the destruction of Jerusalem (C.E. 70) are strong evidences for a pre–C.E. 62 authorship.

19. John Gager, *The Origins of Anti-Semitism: Attitudes Toward Judaism in Pagan and Christian Antiquity* (New York: Oxford University Press, 1985, 184–185).

20. Ibid., 175. Gager points out that among the early principle supporters of Paul were Marcion (who rejected the Old Testament outright), and many of the Gnostics, i.e., Valentinus, Basilides, and Naassners, who, generally, were not supporters of Judaism. The Gnostic texts that either repeat the charge of deicide or are polemical in their treatment of the Jewish people include *The Gospel of Peter* (mid 2nd century), *The Gospel of Nicodemus* (aka *The Acts of Pilate*; 3rd century), *The Acts of Paul* (mid 2nd century), *Acts of the Holy Apostles Peter and Paul* (2nd century), *The Acts of Andrew and Matthew* (late 2nd century), *The Acts of John* (early 3rd century), *Acts and Martyrdom of the Holy Apostle Andrew* (3rd century), *The Acts of Philip* (4th century), *The Acts of Barnabas* (5th century), *Acts of the Holy Apostle and Evangelist John the Theologian*, *The Revelation of Paul*, *The Revelation of Stephen*, *Heracleon* (fragments from his commentary on the Gospel of John; late 2nd century), *The Crucifixion Hymn*, and *The Apocalypse of the Virgin*.

21. This is not the earliest example, for Jesus, in Jhn 5.45–47, tells the Jewish leaders that Moses accuses them of unbelief.

22. Mt 11.17 (cf. Lk 7.32), Mt 13.14–15 (cf. Mk 4.12; Lk 8.10), Mt 15.7–9 (cf. Mk 7.6–7), Mt 21.42 (cf. Mk 12.10–11; Lk 20.17), and Jhn 12.38–40 are a few examples of this practice.

23. Rom 10.21 and Rom 11.8–10 are two examples.

24. The Venerable Bede is only one of many early Christian authors who not only believed that Jesus was the chief cornerstone of the text in Ps, but that "the builders were the Jews, while all the Gentiles remained in the wasteland of idols." Bede, *Commentary on the Acts of the Apostles 4.11*.

25. John Chrysostom, *Homilies on the Acts of Apostles*, 11.
26. Ibid.
27. Arator, *On the Acts of the Apostles*, 1.
28. Thayer, *A Greek-English Lexicon of the New Testament*, 619.
29. Ibid., 619–620.
30. See Acts 13.46; Rom 1.16; and 2.9, 10.
31. Hagner writes that "many have argued that the passage was not written by Paul, but constitutes a later addition to the authentic epistle." Hagner, "Paul's Quarrel with Judaism," 130–131. See also n.9 of Hagner's article on p. 131.
32. Setzer, *Jewish Responses to Early Christians*, 39.
33. Hagner, "Paul's Quarrel with Judaism," 149.
34. Ibid., 149, 150.
35. Thayer, *A Greek-English Lexicon of the New Testament*, 301.
36. See Acts 3.17–21.
37. See Acts 3.25–26.
38. The promise to which Peter is referring here is not clear. He may be referring to the promise made to Abraham in Gen 15.5, the one of which he reminded his hearers from the prophet Joel (ch.2.28–32) or the "gift of the Holy Spirit" mentioned in v.38.
39. Interestingly, Thayer says that this ignorance is akin to "moral blindness." Thayer, *A Greek-English Lexicon of the New Testament*, 9.
40. Ambrosiaster, *Commentary on Paul's Epistles*.
41. Paul certainly suggests this in Rom 5–8. See specifically ch. 6.1–14.
42. Douglas R.A. Hare, "The Rejection of the Jews in the Synoptic Gospels and Acts," in *AntiSemitism and the Foundations of Christianity*, ed. Alan T. Davies (New York: Paulist Press, 1979), 30.
43. Ambrosiaster, *Commentary on Paul's Epistles*.
44. Theodoret of Cyr, *Interpretation of the Letter to the Romans*.
45. Ibid.
46. Chrysostom, *Homilies on Romans*, 19.
47. Pelagius, *Pelagius's Commentary on Romans*.
48. Origen, *On First Principles*, 4.2.6.
49. Origen, *Commentary on the Epistle to the Romans*.
50. Eusebius of Caesarea, *Proof of the Gospel*, 2.3.
51. Augustine, *The City of God*, 17.5.
52. Theodoret of Cyr, Interpretation of the Letter to the Romans.
53. Pelagius, *Pelagius's Commentary on Romans*.
54. Diodore, *Pauline Commentary from the Greek Church*.
55. Ambrosiaster, *Commentary on Paul's Epistles*.
56. Ibid.
57. Pelagius, *Pelagius's Commentary on Romans*.
58. Origen, *Commentary on Paul's Epistles*.

Chapter 4
Conclusion

The history of Christianity is a history of conflict, and the first chapters of that conflict were written during the life and ministry of Jesus Himself. Jesus was never seemingly mindful about who He spoke to and with as He grew in His own self-understanding. This study has demonstrated that He chose the self-identifying term "Son of Man" more often then any of the others.[1] Jesus could have used other terms to describe Himself, even using terms less inflammatory. When He was not referring to Himself as the "Son of Man," He was often being referred to as the "Son of God," or the "Christ." The Jewish leaders and others heard Him refer to Himself as "the bread of Life," "the water of life," and "the light of the world." As one might expect, these self-designations led to conflicts between He and the Jewish leaders.

These, appointed and accepted leaders of the Jewish people, eventually, according to the canonical gospel accounts, began to accuse Jesus of blasphemy. When He declared that the "Son of Man" (Jhn 8.28) was unspeakable "I AM" (v.58) of the Tanakh, "they took up stones to throw at Him" (v.59).

Therefore, His reinterpretation of the role and story of the Messiah aside, He was claiming to be God, and this caused many to react with horror and amazement. The writers of the canonical gospels, reflecting on these events years and years later, view the attempts to silence Jesus as motivated by Satan and the Jewish leaders to be in league with demonic forces. The charges and counter charges between Jesus and the Jewish leaders continued to escalate until it lead to the crucifixion of Jesus. In the gospel accounts, the role of different groups of the Jewish community are painted as culpable, and by the time the gospels are finally put to paper, there was a growing consensus among Christians that Jesus was in fact very God. Therefore, for these Christians, the people responsible for the crucifixion of Jesus were guilty of deicide.

However, clear evidence of hostility and even hatred does not automatically translate to anti-Semitism or even anti-Judaism. Even though the writers of the canonical gospels clearly distrusted the Jewish leaders, they do not put into the mouth of Jesus any sweeping condemnation of the Jewish faith, nor are the Jewish people portrayed as helplessly lost or hopelessly ignorant. What we do see is a continued reluctance of the Jewish leaders to believe the claims of Jesus to be the Messiah/God. What we hear in the New Testament is one side of a conflict based on frustration. For the Jewish leaders' part, they were frustrated that the unsanctioned teachings and miracles of Jesus were causing people to follow Him to perdition. For Jesus and His followers, they were frustrated that the clear evidence of the truthfulness of the claims of Jesus to be the Messiah and even God incarnate were being ignored by the religious leaders. The two sides eventually condemned each other, but the condemnations soon were globalized, and the rejection of Jesus was just the latest and greatest rejection of messengers sent by God to rescue His people from sin and themselves. Not only did they kill earlier prophets, they have now killed God. They were guilty of deicide.

The enormity of the crucifixion began to be articulated in the book of Acts and in the epistles, but for our purposes, it may be more instructive to pay attention to what is not heard as well as what is heard. What is heard in Acts and the epistles, either through intimation or directly, is that the Jewish faith is now both superfluous and superseded. It is perhaps in the Epistle to the Hebrews that is found the strongest argument that what as once given to the Hebrew people, is now given to the Christians. Heb 8.11–15 reads,

> But Christ came as High Priest of the good things to come, with the greater and more perfect tabernacle not made with hands, that is, not of this creation. Not with the blood of goats and calves, but with His own blood He entered the Most Holy Place once for all, having obtained eternal redemption. For if the blood of bulls and goats and the ashes of a heifer, sprinkling the unclean, sanctifies for the purifying of the flesh, how much more shall the blood of Christ, who through the eternal Spirit offered Himself without spot to God, purge your conscience from dead works to serve the living God. And for this reason He is the Mediator of the new covenant, by means of death, for the redemption of the transgressions under the first covenant, that those who are called may receive the promise of the eternal inheritance.

It is the Apostle Paul who spends the most time discussing the relative merits of the law as a means of salvation vs. the grace that comes through the death of Jesus. In Rom 3.20 he writes, "Therefore, by the deeds of the Law no flesh will be justified in His sight, for by the law is the knowledge of sin."[2] I suppose that it is impossible to be totally objective when discussing the possibility of New Testament anti-Judaism, but it seems that the New Testament writers are not condemning Judaism but saying that it has been replaced by Christianity.

Christians are the new Israel. The sons of Abraham are those who have faith in Jesus Christ. Jesus is the great High Priest, and He is the lamb of offering, and as the Christians continued to think about the history of God and God's people, they conclude that much of the history of Israel was for their (Christians) benefit. The law was given to lead us to Christ; the sacrifices were types of Christ as the great ante-type.

Of course, all of this is from the Christian perspective. However, it is difficult to imagine that Paul, with his extensive training at the feet of the rabbis, would have a complete misunderstanding of how the law was viewed, and the purposes of the sacrifices at the temple, and the meanings of the Torah, and it is Paul, more than any other canonical writer who explains the meaning of the Christ event vis-à-vis Judaism. Therefore, it is not the Tanakh, the basis of Judaism, that is being rejected, but the Jewish interpretation of the Tanakh. If that can be considered anti-Judaism, then the New Testament is guilty of anti-Judaism.

Finally, the question of New Testament anti-Semitism is something quite different, and I am afraid that many historians and theologians have read second, third, fourth, and fifth century Christian documents, which are patently anti-Semitic, back into the New Testament. The motives assigned to the Jewish leaders are often asides written by the writers of the gospels, but they are not based on any evidence that is acceptable. "The hated Jews killed our Lord, so they must have been plotting to kill Him all along." Paul's railings against the law came to be seen as railings against the Jews, and we cannot discount the historical phenomenon of *argumentum ad hominem* (the literary equivalent of "piling on").

Therefore, the best way to justify acts of violence, either physical, legal, economic, or social against any group of people is to appeal to the God and sacred literature of your intended audience. If you can cause them to believe that there is evidence from their sacred literature that, because of past sins, the target of the aggression is blessed by God, then there is no compunction not to engage in these acts of violence.

This has been our history, but it is a history that is both shameful and full of innocent blood. And if we believe in a judgment from God, we must seriously consider the judgment that will fall on us if we continue to allow this history to repeat itself.

Notes

1. Jesus is referred to by a myriad of names in the New Testament, and in the gospels alone they range from God's "beloved Son (Mk 1.11) to the "Way" (Jhn 14.6).

2. The ancient argument whether Paul is speaking of the Torah or the Decalogue is of no consequence, for it is the concept of "law" as a means of salvation that is the heart of the discussion.

Bibliography

Ancient Texts

Gnostic

Acts and Martyrdom of the Holy Apostle Andrew (pre-5th c.)
Acts of Andrew and Matthew (mid 2nd c.)
Acts of Barnabas (5th c.)
Acts of the Holy Apostle and Evangelist John the Theologian
Acts of the Holy Apostles Peter and Paul
Acts of John (pre-5th c.)
Acts of Paul (late 2nd c.)
Acts of Philip
Apocalypse of the Virgin
Gospel of Nicodemus (aka *Acts of Pilate*; 3rd c.)
Gospel of Peter (early 2nd c.)
Heracleon, *Fragments from his Commentary on John*
Revelation of Paul
Revelation of Stephen (late 4th–early 5th c.)

Catholic, Apocryphal, and Pseudepigraphical

Alexander of Alexandria, (fl. 312–338), On the Soul and Body and the Passion of the Lord
Ambrose (c.339–397), Exposition of the Gospel of Luke
———, Letter 21
Ambrosiaster (4th c.), Commentary on Paul's Epistles

Arator (6th c.), On the Acts of the Apostles
Augustine (354–430), The City of God
———, Grace and Free Will
———, Letter 149
———, On Jews and Judaism
———, Reply to Faustus
———, Sermon 91
Bede (c. 673–735), Commentary on the Acts of the Apostles
Cassian, John (c. 360–c. 435), The Third Conference of Abbot Chaeremon
Chrysostom, John (c. 347–407), Eight Homilies Against the Jews
———, The Gospel of Matthew, Homily 86
———, Homilies on the Acts of the Apostles
———, Homilies on Galatians
———, Homilies on Romans
Commodianus (mid 3rd c.), The Instructions of Commodianus in Favour of Christian Discipline: Against the Gods of the Heathens
Cyprian of Carthage (200–258), Three Testimonies Against the Jews
Cyril of Alexandria (d. 444), Commentary on Luke, Homily 122
———, Commentary on Luke, Homily 152
———, Explanation of the Letter to the Romans
Diadore, Pauline Commentary from the Greek Church
Ephrem the Syrian (c. 306–373), Commentary on Taitian's Diatessaron
Epistle of Barnabas (late 1st–early 2nd c.)
Eusebius of Caesarea (c. 260–c. 340), Ecclesiastical History
———, Proof of the Gospel
Hippolytus of Rome (170–236), Expository Treatise Against the Jews
———, Refutation of All Heresies
Irenaeus (c. 130–c. 200), Against Heresy
Jerome (c. 342–420), Epistle to the Ephesians
Justin Martyr (c. 100–c. 165), Dialogue with Trypho
Mathetes (c. 130), The Epistle of Mathetes to Diognetus
Melito of Sardis (late 2nd c.), On Pascha
Novatian (d. 257), On Jewish Meats
Origen (c. 185–c. 254), Against Celsus
———, Commentary on the Epistle to the Romans
———, Commentary on Matthew
———, Commentary on Paul's Epistles
———, On First Principles
Pelagius (d. c. 418), Pelagius's Commentary on Romans
Pseudo-Clementine Literature (early 3rd c.), Recognitions
[Pseudo-]Constantius, The Holy Letter of St. Paul to the Romans
Severus, Bishop of Al-Ushmunain (fl. 10th c.), The Legend of Christ's Priest-hood
Tertullian (c. 160–c. 225), Against Marcion
———, An Answer to the Jews
———, Apology
Testament of the Twelve Patriarchs (c.190)
Theodoret of Cyr (c. 393–c. 466), Interpretation of the Letter to the Romans

Modern Authors

Alexander, Philip S. "The 'Parting of the Ways' from the Perspective of Rabbinic Judaism." In *Jews and Christians: The Parting of the Ways, A.D. 70 to 135*, ed. James D. G. Dunn, 1-25. Grand Rapids, MI: William B. Eerdmans Publishing Company, 1992.

Alfonsi, Petrus. *Dialogue Against the Jew*. Translated by Irven M. Resnick. *Fathers of the Church Mediaeval* Continuation 8. Washington, D.C.: Catholic University of America Press, 2006.

Almog, Shmuel, ed. *AntiSemitism Through the Ages*. New York: Pergamon Press, 1988.

Arnal, William E., and Michel Desjardins. *Whose Historical Jesus?* Waterloo, Ont: Published by Canadian Corporation for Studies in Religion by Wilfrid Laurier University Press, 1997.

Aviam, Mordechai. *Jews, Pagans and Christians in the Galilee: 25 Years of Archaeological Excavations and Surveys: Hellenistic to Byzantine Periods. Land of Galilee 1*. Rochester, NY: University of Rochester Press, 2004.

Baum, Gregory. Introduction to *Faith and Fratricide: The Theological Roots of Anti-Semitism*, by Rosemary Ruether. Minneapolis, MN: Seabury Press, 1974.

Bockmuehl, Markus. *Jewish Law in Gentile Churches: Halakah and the Beginning of Christian Public Ethics*. Grand Rapids, MI: Baker Book House, 2003.

Boksar, B. M. "Messianism, the Exodus Pattern, and Early Rabbinical Judaism." In *The Messiah: Developments in Earliest Judaism and Christianity*, ed. James Charlesworth, 239–260. Minneapolis, MN: Fortress Press, 1992.

Borg, Marcus, ed. *The Lost Gospel Q: The Original Sayings of Jesus*. Berkeley, CA: Ulysses Press, 1996.

Brueggemann, Walter. *Worship in Ancient Israel: An Essential Guide*. Nashville, TN: Abingdon Press, 2005.

Chanes, Jerome A. *Antisemitism: A Reference Handbook*. Santa Barbara, CA: ABC-CLIO, Inc., 2004.

Charlesworth, James H. *Jews and Christians: Exploring the Past, Present, and Future*. New York: Crossroad Press, 1990.

———, ed. *The Messiah: Developments in Earliest Judaism and Christianity*. Minneapolis, MN: Fortress Press, 1992.

Chilton, Bruce. "Jesus and the Question of Anti-Semitism." In *Anti-Semitism and Early Christianity: Issues of Polemic and Faith*, ed. Craig A. Evans and Donald A. Hagner, 39–54. Minneapolis, MN: Fortress Press, 1993.

———. *Redeeming Time: The Wisdom of Ancient Jewish and Christian Festal Calendars*. Peabody, MA: Hendrickson Publishers, Inc., 2002.

Chilton, Bruce D. and Jacob Neusner. *Classical Christianity and Rabbinic Judaism: Comparing Theologies*. Grand Rapids, MI: Baker Academic–Baker Publishing Group, 2004.

Collins, John. "Messianism in the Maccabean Period." In *Judaisms and Their Messiahs at the Turn of the Christian Era*, eds. Jacob Neusner, William Scott Green, and Ernest S. Frerichs, 97-110. New York: Cambridge University Press, 1987.

Cook, M. J. "Anti-Judaism in the New Testament." *Union Seminary Quarterly Review* 38 (1983): 125-137.

Crossan, John Dominic. *Who Killed Jesus? Exposing the Roots of Anti-Semitism in the Gospel Story of the Death of Jesus*. San Francisco, CA: Harper-SanFrancisco, 1995.

Davies, Alan T., ed. *AntiSemitism and the Foundations of Christianity*. New York: Paulist Press, 1979.

DeSilva. David A. *An Introduction to the New Testament: Contexts, Methods and Ministry Formation.* Downers Grove, IL: InterVarsity Press, 2004.

Dunn, James D. G., ed. *Jews and Christians: The Parting of the Ways, A.D. 70 to 135.* Grand Rapids, MI: Eerdmans Publishing, 1992.

Ehrman, Bart D. *The New Testament: A Historical Introduction to the Early Christian Writings.* New York: Oxford University Press, 2000.

Ellis, E. Earle. "Biblical Interpretation in the New Testament Church." In *Mikra: Text, Translation, Reading and Interpretation of the Hebrew Bible in Ancient Judaism and Early Christianity*, ed. Martin Jan Mulder, 653–90. Philadelphia, PA: Fortress Press, 1988.

Ettinger, Shmuel. "Jew-Hatred in its Historical Context." In *Antisemitism Through the Ages*, ed. Shmuel Almog, 1–12. New York: Pergamon Press, 1988.

Evans, Craig A., and Donald A. Hagner, eds. *Anti-Semitism and Early Christianity: Issues of Polemic and Faith.* Minneapolis, MN: Fortress Press, 1993.

Feldman, L. H. "Is the New Testament Anti-Semitic." *Humanities* 21 (1987): 1–14.

Finkelstein, Norman G. *Beyond Chutzpah: On the Misuse of Anti-Semitism and the Abuse of History.* Berkeley, CA: University of California Press, 2005.

Freudmann, Lillian C. *AntiSemitism in the New Testament.* Lanham, MD: University Press of America, 1994.

Fricke, Weddig. *The Court Martial of Jesus: A Christian Defends the Jews Against the Charge of Deicide.* New York: Grove Weidenfeld, 1987.

Gager, John G. *The Origins of Anti-Semitism: Attitudes Toward Judaism in Pagan and Christian Antiquity.* New York: Oxford University Press, 1985.

Gaston, Loyd. "Paul and the Torah." In *AntiSemitism and the Foundations of Christianity*, ed. Alan Davies, 48-71. New York: Paulist Press, 1979.

Griffith-Jones, Robin. *The Gospel According to Paul: The Creative Genius Who Brought Jesus to the World.* New York: HarperSanFrancisco, 2004.

Gross, Abraham. *Spirituality and Law: Courting Martyrdom in Christianity and Judaism.* Studies in Judaism. Lanham, MD: University Press of America, 2005.

Haacker, Klaus. *The Theology of Paul's Letter to the Romans.* Cambridge, MA: Cambridge University Press, 2003.

Hagner, Donald A. "Paul's Quarrel with Judaism." In *Anti-Semitism and Early Christianity: Issues of Polemic and Faith*, ed. Craig A. Evans and Donald A. Hagner, 128–50. Minneapolis, MN: Fortress Press, 1993.

Hare, Douglas R. A. "The Rejection of the Jews in the Synoptic Gospels and Acts." In *AntiSemitism and the Foundations of Christianity*, ed. Alan T. Davies, 27–47. New York: Paulist Press, 1979.

Hayes, Christine E. *Gentile Impurities and Jewish Identities: Intermarriage and Conversion from the Bible to the Talmud.* Oxford: Oxford University Press, 2002.

Herr, Moshe David. "The Sages' Reaction to Antisemitism in the Hellenistic-Roman World." In *Antisemitism Through the Ages*, ed. Shmuel Almog, 27-38. New York: Pergamon Press, 1988.

Jacobson, Arland Dean. *The First Gospel: An Introduction to Q.* Sonoma, CA: Polebridge Press, 1991.

Johnson, L. T. "The New Testament's Anti-Jewish Slander and the Conventions of Ancient Polemic." *Journal of Biblical Literature* 108 (1989): 419–441.

Johnson, William H. "Was Paul the Founder of Christianity?" *Princeton Theological Review* V (1907): 398-422.

Kavka, Martin. *Jewish Messianism and the History of Philosophy.* Cambridge, MA: Cambridge University Press, 2004.

Klausner, Joseph. *The Messianic Idea in Israel*. New York: Macmillan Co., 1955.

Kloppenborg, John S. *The Formation of Q: Trajectories in Ancient Wisdom Collections*. Philadelphia, PA: Fortress Press, 1987.

———. *Q Parallels: Synopsis, Critical Notes, and Concordance*. Sonoma, CA: Polebridge Press, 1988.

Kolatch, Rabbi Yonatan. *Traditional Jewish Bible Commentary From the First Through Tenth Centuries*. Masters of the Word 1. Jersey City, NJ: Ktav Publishing House, 2006.

Levine, Amy-Jill. *Anti-Judaism and the Gospels*, ed. William R. Farmer. Harrisburg, PA: Trinity Press International, 1999.

———. *The Misunderstood Jew: The Church and the Scandal of the Jewish Jesus*. San Francisco, CA: HarperSanFrancisco, 2006. Levine, Amy-Jill, Dale C. Allison, Jr., and John Dominic Crossan, eds. *The Historical Jesus in Contest*. Princeton, NJ: Princeton University Press, 2006.

Ludemann, Gerd. *Paul: The Founder of Christianity*. Amhurst, NY: Prometheus Books, 2002.

Mack, Burton. *The Lost Gospel: The Book of Q and Christian Origins*. San Francisco, CA: Harper San Francisco, 1993.

McKnight, Scott "A Loyal Critic: Matthew's Polemic with Judaism in Theological Perspective." In *Anti-Semitism and Early Christianity: Issues of Polemic and Faith*, ed. Craig A. Evans and Donald A. Hagner, 55-79. Minneapolis, MN: Fortress Press, 1993.

———. *The Social and Ethnic Dimensions of Matthean Salvation History*. Lewiston, NY: Mellon Press, 1988.

Meagher, John C. "As the Twig Was Bent: Antisemitism in Greco-Roman and Earliest Christian Times." In *AntiSemitism and the Foundations of Christianity*, ed. Alan T. Davies, 1-26. New York: Paulist Press, 1979.

Michael, Robert. *A Concise History of American Antisemitism*. Lanham, MD: Rowman and Littlefield, 2005.

Mulder, Martin Jan, ed. *Mikra: Text, Translation, Reading and Interpretation of the Hebrew Bible in Ancient Judaism and Early Christianity*. Peabody, MA: Hendrickson Publishers, 2004.

Neusner, Jacob. *Judaism in the Beginning of Christianity*. Philadelphia, PA: Fortress Press, 1984.

Nickelsburg, George W. "Resurrection, Immortality, and Eternal Life in Inter-testamental Judaism and Early Christianity." *Harvard Theological Studies*, 56. Expanded ed. Cambridge, MA: Harvard University Press, 2006.

Oden, Thomas C., gen. ed. *Ancient Christian Commentary on Scripture*. Vol. Ib, *Matthew 14–28*, ed. by Manlio Simonetti. Downers Grove, IL: InterVarsity Press, 2002.

———. *Ancient Christian Commentary on Scripture*. Vol. II, *Mark*, ed. by Thomas C. Oden and Christopher A. Hall. Downers Grove, IL: InterVarsity Press: 1998.

———. *Ancient Christian Commentary on Scripture*. Vol. III, *Luke*, ed. by Arthur A. Just, Jr. Downers Grove, IL: InterVarsity Press, 2003.

———. *Ancient Christian Commentary on Scripture*. Vol. V, *Acts*, ed. by Francis Martin. Downers Grove, IL: InterVarsity Press, 2006.

———. *Ancient Christian commentary on Scripture*. Vol. VI, *Romans*, ed. by Gerald Bray. Downers Grove, IL: InterVarsity Press, 1998.

———. *Ancient Christian Commentary on Scripture*. Vol. VIII, *Galatians, Ephesians, Philippians*, ed. by Mark J. Edwards. Downers Grove, Il: InterVarsity Press, 1999.

---. *Ancient Christian Commentary on Scripture*. Vol. X, *Hebrews*, ed. by Erik M. Heen, and Philip D. W. Krey. Downers Grove, IL: InterVarsity Press, 2005.

Pagels, Elaine, and Karen L. King. *Reading Judas: The Gospel of Judas and the Shaping of Christianity*. New York: Viking Press, 2007.

Perry, Marvin, and Frederick M. Schweitzer. *Antisemitism: Myth and Hate from Antiquity to the Present*. New York: Palgrave Macmillan, 2002.

Rokeah, David. "The Church Fathers and the Jews in Writings Designed for Internal and External Use." In *Antisemitism through the Ages*, ed. Shmuel Almog, 39-69. New York: Pergamon Press, 1988.

Ruether, Rosemary. *Faith and Fratricide: The Theological Roots of Anti-Semitism*. Minneapolis, MN: Seabury Press, 1974.

Scott, James M. *Geography in Early Judaism and Christianity: The Book of Jubilees*. New York: Cambridge University Press, 2002.

Schoeps, H. J. *Paul: The Theology of the Apostle in the Light of Jewish Religious History*. Translated by H. Knight. Philadelphia, PA: Westminster Press, 1961.

Schweizer, Eduard. *A Theological Introduction to the New Testament*. Translated by O. C. Dean, Jr. Nashville, TN: Abingdon Press, 1991.

Segal, Eliezer. *From Sermon to Commentary: Expounding the Bible in Talmudic Babylonia*. Studies in Christianity and Judaism. Waterloo, Ontario: Wilfrid Laurier University Press, 2005.

Setzer, Claudia. *Jewish Responses to Early Christians: History and Polemics, 30–150 C.E.* Minneapolis, MN: Fortress Press, 1994.

Sevenster, Jan Nicolaas. *The Roots of Pagan Anti-Semitism in the Ancient World*. Leiden, Holland: Brill, 1975.

Shapiro, Lamed. *The Cross and Other Jewish Stories*. Edited by Leah Garrett. New Yiddish Library Series. New Haven, CT: Yale University Press, 2007.

Sheleff, Leon. *In the Shadows of the Cross: Jewish-Christian Relations Through the Ages*. London: Vallentine Mitchell, 2004.

Siker, Jeffrey S. *Disinheriting the Jews: Abraham in Early Christian Controversy*. Louisville, KY: Westminster/John Knox Press, 1991.

Stern, Menahem. "Antisemitism in Rome." In *Antisemitism Through the Ages*, ed. Shmuel Almog, 13–25. New York: Pergamon Press, 1988.

Taubes, Jacob. *The Political Theology of Paul*. Edited by Aleida Assmann, et al. Trans. Dana Hollander. Stanford, CA: Stanford University Press, 2004.

Thayer, Joseph Henry, trans. *A Greek-English Lexicon of the New Testament*. Grand Rapids, MI: Zondervan Publishing House, 1889.

Townsend, John T. "The Gospel of John and the Jews: The Story of a Religious Divorce." In *AntiSemitism and the Foundation of Christianity*, ed. Alan Davies, 72–97. New York: Paulist Press, 1979.

Vaage, Leif. *Galilean Upstarts: Jesus' First Followers According to Q*. Valley Forge, PA: Trinity Press International, 1994.

---, ed. *Religious Rivalries in the Early Roman Empire and the Rise of Christianity*. Waterloo, Ont: Published for the Canadian Corporation for Studies in Religion by Wilfrid Laurier University Press, 2006.

Van Landingham, Chris. *Judgment and Justification in Early Judaism and the Apostle Paul*. Peabody, MA: Hendrickson Publishers, 2006.

Wenham, David. *Paul, Follower of Jesus or Founder of Christianity*. Grand Rapids, MI: Wm. B. Eerdmans, 1995.

Wyschogrod, Michael. *Abraham's Promise: Judaism and Jewish-Christian Relations*. Edited by R. Kendall Soulen. Grand Rapids, MI: William B. Eerdmans, 2004.

Yee, Tet-Lim N. *Jews, Gentiles and Ethnic Reconciliation: Paul's Jewish Iden-tity and Ephesians*. Society for New Testament Studies. Cambridge, MA: Cambridge University Press.

Yoder, John Howard. *The Jewish-Christian Schism Revisited*. Grand Rapids, MI: William B. Eerdmans, 2003.

Zucker, David J. *The Torah: An Introduction for Christians and Jews*. New York: Paulist Press, 2005.

Index

Scripture Index

Tanakh

Gen **28**, 10
Ex **6**, 15
Lev **4**, 2; **16**, 71
I Sam **24**, 2
2 Kings **14**, 33
I Chron **16**, 2
Ps **16**, 60; **84**, 2; **89**, 2; **105**, 2; **110**, 60; **118**, 22, 61
Isa **45**, 2; **29**, 18
Jer **30**, 6
Joel **2**, 60
Zech **13**, 23

New Testament

Mt **1**, xiii, xiv; **5**, xi; **8**, 6, 8, 10, 12, 16; **9**,xiv, 9, 10, 12, 34 (2), 45; **10**, xiii; **11**, xiii, 6, 7, 10, 15; **12**, xi, 6 (3), 7, 9, 10 (3), 16 (2), 17, 20, 32, 33; **13**, 9, 20, 32, 34; **16**, xiv, 9(2), 21(2), 32, 33 (2); **17**,xiv, 7, 9, 24, 35; **18**, xiii; **19**, 9, 26, 33, 34; **20**, xiv, 9(2), 22, 28,(2), 34, 35 (2), 58; **21**, xi, 22; **22**, xi, xiii, 6, 60; **23**, xi; **26**, xi (2), xiv, 9, 10, 21, 23, 30, 31 (4), 33, 58 (3) **27**, xiv, xv, 31 (3), 58 (2); **28**, xiii, xv
Mk **2**, xi, 9, 10 (2), 12, 16, 34; **3**,10; **8**, 9, 21, 33; **9**, 9, 24, 35; **10**, 9, 22, 26, 28, 33, 35 (2), 58; **12**, xi (2), 6, 9; **14**, xi, 9,30, 31(4), 33, 45, 58 (2); **15**, 31(3), 58
Lk **4**, xi; **5**, 10, 12, 34; **6**, 10, 16; **7**, 15, 26 (2); **8**, 26 (2); **9**, 9 (2), 10, 12, 21, 24, 33, 35; **10**, xi;

11, 6, 9, 10 (2), 20, 33; **17**, 6, 7, 9, 10, 22, 25, 26, 33, 35; **18**, 9 (2), 26 (2), 28, 33 (2), 35 (2), 58; **19**, 9, 10; **20**, xi, 6; **22**, xi, 9 (2), 30, 31 (3), 33, 58 (2); **23**, xiv, 31 (2), 58
Jhn **1**, xvi, 9, 10, 32; **2**, xi; **3**, xi, xiii,10, 11, 22, 29, 32, 34, 56; **4**, xvi; **5**, xi (2), xvi, 10, 12, 34 (2), 58 (3); **6**, xi, xiii, xvi, 10, 14, 34, 35; **7**, xi, xii, 58 (3); **8**, viii, xvi (2),10, 15, 24, 25, 34, 35, 58, 81; **9**, 10, 25, 33; **10**, 22, 23, 45; **11**, 58; **12**, 10 (3), 29, 34; **13**, 9, 29, 33; **17**, xiii; **18**, xi, 58 (2); **19**, 31, 58; **20**, xiii
Acts **1**, 70; **2**, 23, 50 (2), 59, 70; **3**, 60, 71 (2); **4**, 50, 60, 61 (2);

5, 62, 72; **7**, 45, 62; **8**, 50; **9**, 44, 47, 48; **10**, 63, 72; **11**, 72; **12**, 44; **13**, 45, 47 (2), 48 (2), 50, 59, 64, 72; **14**, 48, 50; **17**, 48 (2), 49, 50 (2); **18**, 45, 49 (2), 50 (3); **19**, 49; **21**, 50
Rom **1**, 73; **2**, 51, 73; **3**, 23, 67, 73 (2), 82; **4**, 67, 73; **5**, 67; **8**, 29, 67 (2); **9**, 51, 73; **10**, 51, 73 (2); **11**, 73, 74, 75
Gal **1**, 67; **2**, 59, 74; **3**, 74; **4**, 67
2 Cor **3**, 51; **5**, 67
Eph **2**, 74; **3**, 74
Phil **2**, xiii
Col **1**, 67; **3**, 74
1 Thess **2**, 46, 65, 66
Heb **8**, 82; **9**, 29, 68
1 Peter **1**, 68 (2)
1 John **2**, 68

Name Index

Alexander, Philip, 3

Boksar, B. M., 5
Borg, Marcus, 6

Chilton, Bruce, xii, xv, 46
Collins, John, 5
Cook, M. J., xvi
Crossan, John Dominic, 55

DeSilva, David A., 6

Ellis, E. Earle, 5
Ettinger, Shmuel, xvii, xviii

Freudmann, Lillian, 2, 3

Gager, John G., 59
Gaston, Loyd, xiv, xvi, xviii
Godhead, Christian, xviii

Hagner, Donald, xix, 46, 47

Hare, Douglas, xv, xvi, 51
Helms, Randal, 6

King, Karen, xii
Klausner, Joseph, 2
Kloppenborg, John S., 6

Matthean Jews, xv
Mcknight, Scott, xv
Meagher, John, xii, xv, xviii, 3

Neusner, Jacob, 2

Pagels, Elaine, xii
Perry, Marvin, xii, 55
Powell, M. A., 6

Rokeah, David, xi
Ruether, Rosemary, xiv, xvi, xvii, xviii, 1
Schoeps, Hans Joachim, 46
Schweitzer, Frederick M., xii, 55

Setzer, Claudia, xv, 19, 66
Sheleff, Leon, xviii, xxii, 2, 3, 57
Stern, Menaham, xxi

Townsend, John T., xvi, xviii

Subject Index

Anti-Judaism, vii, xii, xv, xvi–xix, 13, 20, 36, 47, 56, 82
Anti-Semitism, vii, xv, xvii–xix, 20, 36, 47, 56, 82

Blasphemy
   Jesus accused of, viii, 11–15, 17, 19, 21, 25, 26, 30
   Jews accused of, 45, 46

Chosen people, xvi, 31, 36, 43
Circumcision, 19

Dead Sea Scrolls, 4
Deicide, viii, xiv, 43, 55, 56–66
Divine Judgment, 20, 26, 27, 28, 32

Elders, 30
Enemies of Jesus (according to the gospel writers)
   Chief Priests, 18, 21, 30
   High Priests, 30
   Judas Iscariot, 31
   Matthean Jews, xv
   Pharisees, xi, xv, 16–19, 25, 26
   Pontius Pilate, 23
   Priests, 18
   Romans, 31
   Sadducees, 18
   Scribes, 17, 18, 19, 21, 30

Food laws, 19

Gnostic writings, 8–9
Heresy, 15
Hermeneutic, viii, xi

Biblical
   Displacement theory, xvi
   Replacement theory, xvi
   Tools
      Exegesis, xii
      Redactors, xv, 21

Incarnation, purposes of
   Atonement for sins, 22, 55
   Crucifixion, viii, xi, xiii, xiv, 19, 21, 22, 28, 29, 43
   Death of Jesus
      Predetermined, 22, 23, 29–31
      Prophesied, 23
   Ransom, 22, 28, 29
   Resurrection, 21, 28, 29
   Salvation of Israel, 43
      In the Epistles, 66–69, 72–76
      In the Book of Acts, 69–72
   Substitution, 21, 28

Jewish Diaspora, xii, 11
Jewish Literature
   Jewish Apocrypha, 3
   Jewish Pseudepigrapha, 3
   Tanakh, xi, xviii, 31
   Targumim, 4
   Torah, viii, xi, 14, 19, 26, 30

Messiah, viii, xiii, xv, 1–17, 18, 20, 21, 27–32, 46

Paul, the Apostle
   Apostle to the gentiles, 47

Founder of Christianity, 47
Preaching in synagogues, 47–50
and the salvation of the Jewish people, 49–50
Attempt to rewrite the history of Israel, 51, 52
Pauline Corpus, possible interpretations of
Systematic alternative to Rabbinic Judaism, 46
Fulfillment of Judaism, 46

Q Gospel, xii, xv, 5–8

Sabbath, xi, 16, 18, 19
Son of Man,
Unique relationship with Heaven, 32
Unique relationship with God, 33
As Judge of Israel and the world, 33
As Savior of Israel and the world, 33–34
As God of Israel and the world, 34
As Self-existent, 35

Temple, 16, 19, 43

About the Author

Dr. Evans and his wife live in Pickerington, Ohio, a suburb of Columbus, Ohio. They have two grown sons.

This is Dr. Evans' second book published by University Press of America. His first book, *Sex and Salvation: Virginity as a Soteriological Paradigm in Ancient Christianity,* explores the emerging issues of gender and sexuality in Christianity in the first six centuries of the Common Era.

Dr. Evans received his B.S. in theology from Columbia Union College in 1976, his M.Div. from Andrews Theological Seminary in 1979, his M.A. in ancient history from The Ohio State University in 1991, and his Ph.D. in intellectual history with a concentration in early Christian theology from The Ohio State University in 1996. Before his current tenure at Payne (1990-2008), he pastored for fifteen years in the Ohio Conference of Seventh-Day Adventists (1976-1977; 1979-1994).

This book grew out of research for his class "History of Conflict between Christianity and Judaism." It was originally intended to be a chapter in an exploration of the issues of early Christian anti-Judaism and anti-Semitism. However, it soon became apparent that an attempt to cover these issues in the New Testament in one chapter was insufficient, and that chapter became this book. Although an exploration of the origins of Christian/Jewish hostility most logically begins with the New Testament, that study is incomplete without looking at what extra-canonical Christian authors in the ancient world (c. 5th C.E.) had to say about the Jewish religion and the Jewish people. That study will be taken up in the forthcoming volume two.

www.ingramcontent.com/pod-product-compliance
Lightning Source LLC
Chambersburg PA
CBHW021834300426
44114CB00009BA/435